Hispanic Families

Critical Issues for Policy and Programs in Human Services

Edited by
Miguel Montiel

COSSMHO®

National Coalition of Hispanic Mental Health
and Human Services Organizations
Washington, D.C.

International Standard Book Number: 0-933084-00-5
Library of Congress Catalog Card Number: 78-73213

Printed in the United States of America

Cover concept by Rodolfo Balli Sanchez
Graphics by Hector de Leon

Special acknowledgment is given to D.J. Curren, Coordinator, Research and Public Information, COSSMHO, for his work in final editing and preparation of this book.

CONTENTS

CONTRIBUTORS

George Thomas Beall
Program Associate
International Center for
  Social Gerontology
Washington, D.C.

Ismael Dieppa, D.S.W.
Professor, Dean
School of Social Work
Arizona State University
Tempe, Arizona

John Florez, M.S.W.
Assistant Professor
Graduate School of Social Work
University of Utah
Salt Lake City, Utah

Rosa C. Marin, D.S.W.
Former Dean
Graduate School of Social Work
University of Puerto Rico
Consultant
Department of Addiction Services
Commonwealth of Puerto Rico
Santurce, Puerto Rico

Miguel Montiel, D.S.W.
Professor
School of Social Work
Arizona State University
Tempe, Arizona

Javier Saenz, Ph.D.
Chairman
Salt Lake Spanish-Speaking Health and
  Mental Health Task Force
Director
Adult Day Care Unit
Granite Community Mental Health Center
Salt Lake City, Utah

Jose Szapocznik, Ph.D.
Department of Psychiatry
University of Miami
Miami, Florida

Fernando Manuel Torres-Gil, Ph.D.
Director, Project MASP
  (Minority Aging and Social Policy)
Director, Recruitment
Andrus Gerontology Center
University of Southern California
Los Angeles, California

Carroll Truss, Ph.D.
Department of Psychology
University of Miami
Miami, Florida

FOREWORD

Today, perhaps more than at any time in recent memory, there is a pronounced upsurge in public and governmental attention to families— their problems, stresses, strengths, and roles in contemporary American society. At the heart of this concern is the growing awareness of the need to strengthen, not weaken, family life and to utilize socio-cultural resources inherent in families to advance important national goals such as the health, mental health, and social responsibility of all citizens.

As part of this national dialogue, COSSMHO—The National Coalition of Hispanic Mental Health and Human Services Organizations is holding the National Hispanic Conference on Families, October 12-15, 1978 in Houston, Texas. This Conference is the first of its kind to examine the current status of Hispanic families in American society and to explore policies, strategies, and actions needed for the future. Its theme and focus—*La Familia*—reflect a fundamental concern and long-standing emphasis among all Hispanics despite our diverse national origins and geographic locations, and are directly responsive to the need for a national focus on Hispanic families, a need repeatedly expressed by participants in COSSMHO's regional conference series and its National Conference on Health and Human Services and by member agencies and individuals throughout COSSMHO's nationwide network.

The publication of this book—examining the historical processes, cultural values, and socio-economic conditions that contribute to the current status of Hispanic families—is thus particularly timely. *La Familia* continues to be our primary unit for preserving, fostering, and strengthen- ing personal and cultural identity, self-esteem, social and personal values and responsibility, and physical and mental well-being. For us Hispanics, the shared experience of *La Familia* is a distinctive bond of unity, one that incorporates both nuclear and extended family members, one that embraces neighbors, friends, and community supports as well, and one that links all together with ties of kinship, mutual respect, and reciprocal support. Its enhancement is clearly a basic point of reference, concern, and action for those of us working in health, mental health, and related human service fields in Cuban, Latino, Mexican American, and Puerto Rican communities.

This collection of papers focuses on selected aspects of the complex, diverse roles and impacts of *La Familia* in Hispanic communities. In particular, it explores their implications for improved social policy and programs that will benefit Hispanic families and those segments of our populations most at risk—low-income families with children, families severely strained by acculturation stresses, our young people, and our elderly. Papers selected for this book were obtained from two sources— some were commissioned for presentation at the National Conference on Health and Human Services previously sponsored by COSSMHO and others were contributed by COSSMHO members engaged in family- oriented and family-significant research. Together, they point to critical issues in theory and practice that must be addressed in shaping services, research, and training most appropriate to the needs and circumstances of Hispanic families. COSSMHO's National Hispanic Conference on Families will further expand and refine the knowledge available on the implications of *La Familia* for social policy and programs in broad areas of concern to our communities—health and mental health, drug and alcohol abuse, welfare, employment, housing, civil rights, juvenile justice, police-community relations, the media, and the special needs of children, youth, and the elderly.

This volume is published by COSSMHO—The National Coalition of Hispanic Mental Health and Human Services Organizations in the interest of achieving the broadest dissemination of the viewpoints, insights, and recommendations contained herein. Under its project entitled "COSSMHO's National Task Force on Mental Health" (Grant No. 5 R01 MH25411-05 from DHEW/PHS/ADAMHA/NIMH), COSSMHO develops and conducts a number of research and dissemination activities related to improved services development and delivery and to public policy dialogue. For their valuable assistance in securing funds to complete this publication and make it widely available in the field, COSSMHO extends special acknowledgment to the following officials of the National Institute of Mental Health: Howard R. Davis, Ph.D., Chief, Mental Health Services Development Branch, and Juan Ramos, Ph.D., Director, Division of Special Mental Health Programs.

J. Julian Rivera
Chairman
Board of Directors
COSSMHO

Preface

Health, mental health, and related human services for Hispanic families have been a favored topic of discussion among Anglo researchers and social scientists for a good many years. Even a cursory review of the literature reveals a variety of strategies proposed to deal with so-called "problem" Hispanic families in the Southwest and on the Eastern Seaboard. Much of the early writings proposed public policy that ran counter to behavior valued by Hispanics. For example, until recently public policy discouraged bilingualism, encouraged segregation, ignored inequality, and maintained welfare rules that disrupted family life. The perspective underlying such policy was detached, corrective, and invariably punitive.

The discussion presented in the papers in this book is different in that nearly all of the authors are Hispanic and their focus of attention is appreciative. While this is significant, the ultimate test is whether Hispanics can articulate and implement strategies that preserve rather than destroy, liberate rather than dominate. It is not unfair, therefore, to judge the papers in this book as to whether or not they offer ideas, insights, and recommendations that are liberating for our Hispanic communities.

The first paper represents a beginning effort to treat the Hispanic populations in the United States in a unified manner. It presents a brief overview of the major historical forces that have brought these populations into proximity with the dominant Anglo society. Although these population groups share some similar characteristics, there are significant historical, geographical, and racial differences among them. The demographic figures lead to the conclusion that, in general, Hispanic families tend to be disproportionately poor, uneducated or undereducated, youthful, and growing at a rate greater than the rest of the population.

In light of the great disparities between Hispanics and the general population, the authors argue for social programs that are selective, rather than universal, in their application. The objective viewpoint of this paper, although an important first step, does not directly address the subjective aspects of Hispanic families. These aspects place Hispanic families as the central actors in their world. A comprehensive and holistic view must give close attention to both perspectives. Another paper, related in outlook and theme, focuses on the largest of the Hispanic population groups in this country—Mexican Americans or Chicanos—and presents a socio-historical overview of their current status and identifies major Chicano academic perspectives that seek to illuminate and interpret that status within the framework of Chicano experience.

The paper by Javier Saenz describes an approach toward instilling and implementing a humanistic perspective in the delivery of human services to Hispanic families. It is based on the author's experience in the successful Minority Human Service Training Program in Salt Lake City, Utah. The purpose of this program is to serve and train people from Spanish-speaking backgrounds, and from other minority and disadvantaged groups, in the mental health and human service fields. To Saenz, humanistic services are those that, at the point of both planning and delivery, respect in practice the cultural identity of the consumer and recognize and maintain the individuality, the uniqueness of the consumer. He notes the existence of public laws on health and mental health which, if utilized properly, can enhance local input and more consumer-sensitive input into the design and implementation of human service delivery systems. The implicit message is that ideas must be merged with action if humanistic services are indeed to become a reality in our communities.

The issue of acculturation among Cuban American families is addressed in the paper by Szapocznik and Truss. Their focus is on a particular sample of mothers; their intent is to identify one process that may help explain how the familial pathology of intergenerational differences in acculturation affects some Cuban mothers and becomes a source of role conflict and role stress that results in their symptomatic behavior, their use and abuse of sedatives and tranquilizers. Their study further identifies a critical area for research on appropriate therapeutic assistance for particular types of families with special needs arising from the Cuban experience in this country.

The vulnerability of the "poorest of the poor" is emphasied in Marin's analysis of characteristics of dependent needy families in San Juan, Puerto Rico. Her discussion, based on a series of studies in which she was actively involved, clarifies how knowledge gained in studies such as these can assist social welfare agencies in working to prevent the occurrence of such conditions or help ameliorate some of the urgent problems that these needy families face.

The health care utilization patterns of Spanish-speaking elderly are examined in the paper by Torres-Gil. His analysis employs a review of the literature as well as selected empirical studies of Mexican American elderly in various settings in the Southwest. He argues that Hispanics need not only a more humane, efficient, and expanded health care delivery system, but also one that recognizes, incorporates, and maintains the subjective coping mechanisms utilized by Hispanic people. His discussion of such coping mechanisms as folk medicine, the family, and religion is of particular importance because of the nature of the existing health care system which tends to exclude the elderly bilingual/bi-cultural person. These coping mechanisms begin to address the subjective aspects of the elderly Hispanic's existence. It is also important to note that, because of the persistent lack of readily available and reliable information on Hispanics and on Hispanic elderly in particular, much of the discussion in the paper must deal exclusively with a few selected studies on elderly Mexican Americans.

As Torres-Gil indicates, the problems faced by Hispanic elderly are basically the result of an insensitive system unable to accommodate their special needs. Further evidence of the systematic difficulties is provided by Beall in his analysis of the responsiveness of Older Americans Act programs to Hispanic and other minority elderly. His paper is enlightening because it documents the prevailing differences between Congressional intent and actual implementation of these programs. Notwithstanding the natural problems inherent in advancing age, Hispanic elderly have shown themselves to be remarkably resilient, and a few profound changes in the system would yield rather dramatic results in the delivery of services to them.

The obstacles facing our youth are not as simple. The Hispanic population is vulnerable, both externally and internally. The paper by Florez identifies some of the major problems facing Hispanic youth and analyzes some of the efforts to resolve them. He offers recommendations to improve the social conditions of Hispanic youth and gives particular attention to the problem of juvenile delinquency as it affects them. He argues that what is needed is not so much a national juvenile delinquency policy, but rather a national family policy "supporting families in carrying out their role of assisting their younger members to function adequately."

The message in all of these papers is that Hispanics are the second largest ethnic minority in the United States today and are projected to be its largest within the next few decades; that Hispanics constitute a disproportionately poor, undereducated, and exceedingly youthful population; that Hispanics underutilize what are already inappropriate services; and that unless something dramatic is done, the future for us does not look promising.

The truth is that, historically, Hispanics have not been involved in the public policy discussions that affect them and that there is much that needs to be learned objectively and subjectively about this complex and diverse population. The social and political influence that we need to mobilize must be tempered with sound judgment. We must remember that many of the problems facing this country today are a result of irresponsible actions motivated by greed, expediency, and ignorance. Action without reflection, just like reflection without action, will result in domestication. The challenge to academics, planners, policy makers, and public officials is to correct the disturbing problems facing large segments of the Hispanic population because these problems affect not only our families and their most vulnerable members, but also the health and integrity of the entire Nation.

Miguel Montiel
Editor

HISPANIC FAMILIES: AN EXPLORATION

Ismael Dieppa and Miguel Montiel

The stress and pressures of American society have probably had a greater impact on Hispanic families* than on any other segment of the population. There are historical, cultural, demographic, social, political, and economic factors supporting the premise that Hispanic families are susceptible to a multitude of pressures, demands, and stresses which are an integral part of their high-risk status.

The growing literature on the status of families in American society today points out a disturbing trend: the increasing disintegration or disorganization of the family unit as the basic institution of socialization. This trend seems most evident in:

- The erosion of the role of the family as other institutions usurp such functions as child rearing and care, transmission of moral and cultural values, and responsibility for emotional growth and development.
- Growing social and health problems which especially affect young children and families—drug and alcohol abuse, child abuse, divorce, juvenile delinquency, school dropouts, malnutrition, and other physical and mental health conditions.
- The high rate of mobility and displacement caused by economic and other structural forces in society and often resulting in the disruption and uprooting of families.

This trend toward disintegration or disorganization is of particular significance to Hispanic families because of societal pressures on them to assimilate and acculturate to an environment that in many respects is alien, often hostile, contradictory, and destructive.

This paper, a beginning effort to study the nature of Hispanic families within the continental United States, first examines some of the racial aspects of the various groups that comprise the U.S. Hispanic population. We focus on three easily identifiable groupings—Mexican Americans, Puerto Ricans, and Cubans—but recognize that there are also significant numbers of persons of Central and South American descent as well as other Spanish origins. Using census data, we examine the number, geographic distribution, language, education, and income characteristics of the above three groups. Next, we explore the principal societal problems which Hispanic families face, not as isolated entities, but within the context of the society in which they live and function. Finally, we discuss key social policy issues and speculate on their impact on Hispanic families. We present premises, facts, ideas, and conclusions in a rather tentative manner. The tentative nature of this paper is guided by our conviction that there is a critical need to go beyond the dearth of research

---

*In this paper the term "Hispanic families" refers to those of Mexican American, Puerto Rican, Cuban, or other Latin American origin or descent who live in the continental United States.

and information available at present. We are currently collaborating in the development of a study and text on the subject of Hispanic families.

A Socio-Historical Perspective

The writing of the socio-history of Hispanic family life within the context of Anglo-American society remains an unfinished task. However, it is important to recognize that there are both common and unique historical elements that enable us to understand the status of Hispanic families in this society.

Mexican Americans and Puerto Ricans represent the two largest groups within this country's Hispanic population. Unlike European immigrants who came here from the mid-19th through the early part of the 20th century, these two groups shared the experience of conquest and annexation as their initial threshold of entry—Mexican Americans as a result of the War of 1846-1848, Puerto Ricans as a result of the Spanish-American War in 1898 (with U.S. citizenship being granted to them in 1917). Although these wars do not completely explain the presence of millions of Hispanics in this country today, they set the stage for future mass migrations of both Mexicans and Puerto Ricans to the United States.

Hernandez (1970) estimates that well over one million Mexican Americans are descendents of Mexicans who resided in the Southwest as far back as 1848. However, two-thirds of the Mexican American population are either recent immigrants or descendents of immigrants who arrived in this country between 1910 and 1960. A number of interrelated factors contributed to this mass migratory movement during that 50-year period. The substantial and more permanent movement of Mexicans to the United States was due to the instability created by the Mexican Revolution of 1910 and the emerging demand for cheap labor in this country. During the 1920s, immigration from Mexico achieved mass proportions— approximately 500,000 persons entered on permanent visas during that decade. The trend was reversed during the Great Depression of the 1930s as mass repatriation and deportation took place (Grebler, 1965). The next phase of Mexican migration occurred during World War II under the *bracero* program. This program, which continued until 1964, led to the large-scale importation of agricultural workers under bilateral agreements between the governments of Mexico and the United States.

After World War II, Puerto Ricans joined Mexicans as a large source of cheap agricultural labor, particularly in the eastern seaboard States. The advent of widespread commercial air travel, the poverty on the island, the demand for labor led to the largest migration of Puerto Ricans to the mainland. Like the Mexicans, Puerto Ricans gradually left the agricultural migrant stream and settled in urban centers.

The period from 1950 through 1959 was characterized by a continuous mass migration of both Mexicans and Puerto Ricans to this country. It was also in the 1950s that "Operation Wetback" was implemented to apprehend and deport illegal aliens. During the first half of the decade, about 3.8 million Mexican aliens were deported (Grebler, 1965). As in the 1930s, family and kinship ties were disrupted by arbitrary repatriations which often included persons with long residence status in this country. However, it is important to realize that migratory movements do not explain either the historical presence of Mexican Americans in the Southwest or their condition of poverty and exploitation. Mexican Americans perceive legal boundaries between Mexico and this country as

2

artificial barriers. The geographic, ecological, and cultural blending of the Southwest with Mexico is perceived as a continuing unity which binds together, as it did prior to 1848, the lives and destiny of a people whose claim to the Southwest is rooted in the land itself.

Due to political upheavals, unfavorable economic conditions, or both, Cubans and other Latin Americans migrated here in search of better living conditions. Beginning in the 1960s, and especially in the period from 1960 to 1962, large numbers of Cuban families resettled in this country under the Cuban Refugee Program. By 1970 there were over 500,000 Cubans in the United States (Conde, 1970).

The migration of Mexicans, Puerto Ricans, Cubans, and other Hispanic groups to this country resulted in the eventual movement of whole families when the head of the household or a younger member migrated first; in many instances, whole families migrated together. Their arrival was characterized by cultural "shock," i.e., the language barrier; different cultural traditions, values, beliefs, and life styles; racial attitudes and discrimination; different institutional systems; and, for many, adaptation from an agrarian or rural environment to an urban environment. Their generally low level of education, inability or limited ability to speak the language, and discrimination in employment relegated them to low-income status and poverty. Even in the case of middle class and professional Cuban families, the head of the household often found only menial jobs.

Hispanic families are characterized by the diversity among and within the various population subgroups and by the common socio-cultural elements which bind them as "Hispanics," "Latinos," or "La Raza." The cultural heritage of Spain, the Spanish language, the Catholic religion, Indo-Hispanic traits and heritage among some, and African-Indo-Hispanic traits and heritage among others have meshed with time to create the Hispanic families of today. Other factors have also influenced the evolution and status of these families: for example, the original insular (island) environment of Puerto Ricans and Cubans; the rural background of many Puerto Ricans, Cubans, and Mexicans who migrated here; the class status of families prior to departure from their country and after their arrival here; and the circumstances of entry, e.g., Puerto Ricans as citizens and Cubans as "legal" refugees while many Mexicans have been considered "illegal aliens."

Although there are variations among Cubans, Mexican Americans, Puerto Ricans, and other Hispanics, there are also shared values and cultural attributes. A report of the Illinois State Advisory Committee to the U.S. Commission on Civil Rights (1974) suggests that the following characteristics are generally found among Hispanic people:

- Orientation toward persons, rather than toward ideas or abstractions.
- Commitment to individual autonomy with the context of familial and traditional Hispanic values.
- Emphasis on the central importance of the family.
- Emphasis on *being*, rather than *doing*.
- Emphasis on the father as main authority figure.

Ramirez and Castaneda (1974) have identified four major value clusters in the "traditional Mexican American culture" which may be, generally

3

speaking, attributed to other Hispanic families: (1) identification with family, community, and ethnic group; (2) personalization of inter-personal relationships; (3) status and role definition in family and community; and (4) Hispanic Catholic ideology.

¿Quiénes Somos? Who Are We?

The Bureau of the Census (1971) conducted a sample survey in November 1969 and calculated that there were approximately 9.2 million persons living in the 50 States and the District of Columbia who identified themselves as being of Spanish origin.* The criteria used to identify this population included Spanish origin, mother tongue, and language usually spoken in the home. Historically, the Hispanic population has been undercounted by the Census Bureau primarily because of the criteria used to identify it.** Hispanics have had little confidence in Census Bureau estimates, and a vigilant watch must be kept to insure an accurate count in the 1980 census. An accurate count is important because the figures derived from it influence decisions on legislative reapportionment and the allocation of public resources.

Recognizing the tendency toward undercounting, one must employ considerable reserve in analyzing and interpreting the available demographic characteristics of the Hispanic population. The figures, however, do provide important insights into the status of Hispanic families. In an effort to present an overview of the socio-economic status of the Hispanic population, we have selected demographic data that point to various key issues facing this population.

According to the census survey previously cited, Hispanics are found in all 50 states and the District of Columbia and can be classified in five major categories:

- *Mexican Americans,* concentrated in five Southwestern States (Arizona, California, Colorado, New Mexico, and Texas), comprising 55 percent of the total national Hispanic population, and young (median age, 17.8 years, compared to 28 years for the rest of the U.S. population).
- *Puerto Ricans,* concentrated on the Eastern Seaboard but rapidly extending to other parts of the country (in particular, the Midwest and the West Coast), comprising 16 percent of the Hispanic

---

*This survey was used for this paper because data in pertinent categories discussed herein are not available in subsequent surveys.

**For example, up until 1930, when the classification of Mexican was used, a standard criterion was the birthplace of the person and his/her parents. In 1940 it was Spanish mother tongue. In 1950 and 1960 it was Spanish surname for the five Southwestern States. This system of counting has made it most difficult to have confidence in the numbers and to make accurate projections about the growth rate of this population. The Census Bureau, after considerable pressure from various groups, has admitted undercounting the Hispanic population. The exact figures for this country's Hispanic population today are not available, but conservative estimates range from 12 to 13 million, while other estimates range from 16 to 23 million, taking into account the 3.2 million Puerto Ricans living on the island, allowing for a heavy undercount of the Cuban population, and acknowledging the presence of several million undocumented Hispanics residing on the U.S. mainland. Dr. Joan Moore, co-author (along with Leo Grebler and Ralph Guzman) of the massive study, *The Mexican American People: The Nation's Second Largest Minority* (Free Press, New York, N.Y., 1970), estimates that Mexican Americans have been undercounted by as much as 15 percent. As evidence, she cites instances during the 1960 census where entire census tracts as well as parts of tracts were left out of the count.

4

population in the continental United States, and also young (median age, 18.3 years).

- *Cubans,* comprising six percent of the Hispanic population and differing in some respects from the previous two categories, e.g., the median age is 28.4 years, a figure that conforms more closely to the median age (28 years) of the total U.S. population.
- *Central and South Americans,* comprising six percent of the Hispanic population and having a median age of 24.4 years.
- *Other Spanish,* accounting for the remaining 17 percent, with a median age of 24 years.

In this section we outline the demographic characteristics of the three easily identifiable groups—Mexican Americans, Puerto Ricans, and Cubans.

Cubans and Puerto Ricans proportionately have a greater percentage of persons born outside the continental United States than do Mexican Americans. For example, although the latter comprise 55 percent of the Nation's total Hispanic population, their percentage of foreign-born is only 18 percent. Among Cubans and Puerto Ricans the percentage of those born outside the continental United States is 81 and 55 percent, respectively.

The data on language and literacy provide some interesting insights into this population, in particular, as these data relate to educational and employment opportunities. The percentage of Hispanics reporting Spanish as a mother language, i.e., the language spoken as a child, ranges from 72 percent for Mexican Americans to 95 percent for Cubans. As a current language, however, the use of Spanish drops considerably, particularly for Mexican Americans, with 47 percent reporting that they speak Spanish at home, while 72 percent of Puerto Ricans and 87 percent of Cubans report doing so.

Again, Cubans are the exception when it comes to education as measured by the number of years in school. Cubans have a median of 12.4 years completed by persons in the 25-34 age group and 10.8 years completed by persons age 35 and older. This is comparable to the general population. The figures for Puerto Ricans and Mexican Americans are considerably below those for the general population, with Mexican Americans having an edge in the 25-34 age group (10.8 years vs. 9.9 years for Puerto Ricans) and Puerto Ricans having a slight edge in the 35+ age group (7.5 years vs. 7.3 years for Mexican Americans). The discrepancy between these two Hispanic groups and the larger population is significant.

The ability to read and write English in a monolingual nation is of primary importance. Ninety-five percent of Mexican Americans and 80.6 percent of Puerto Ricans between ages 10 and 24 report they are literate in English, while 81.1 percent of Cubans and persons of Central or South American origin in this age group so report. The situation for persons over age 25 is serious for these Hispanic groups, with the comparable percentages being 72, 72, and 60, respectively.

Mexican Americans and Puerto Ricans are concentrated in the lower echelons of the employment sector, with over 60 percent in blue collar jobs that are *not* the choice industrial jobs that pay wages comparable to middle class earnings. Less than 20 percent of Mexican Americans and Puerto Ricans have white collar jobs.

Family median income for all three groups is considerably below the reported median income of $7,894 for the total population in November 1969. Puerto Ricans had the lowest median income of the three major Hispanic groups—$4,969. When one realizes that Hispanic families are considerably larger than those in the general population, these figures are even more significant.

Problems and Issues

Poverty, and everything it creates, are the most serious problems facing Hispanic families in the United States. The high birth rate and youthfulness of the Mexican American and Puerto Rican populations, viewed in the context of their poverty and low educational attainment, point toward some distressing projections. An unskilled and poorly educated (or miseducated) population in a highly industrialized society can expect serious problems now and in the future.

A full understanding of the problems confronting Hispanic families requires an analysis of their objective status (health, education, income, etc.) in the context of their history as well as their societal context. Government and the demands of its various agencies, the mass media, religion, and numerous formal and informal associations must also be included in such an analysis. Thus far, the literature, developed for the most part by non-Hispanics, has neglected the historical and institutional forces and, as a consequence, has placed the burden of responsibility solely on the family. The implications of this stance for intervention programs are profound. For example, this stance has led to special education and achievement motivation programs rather than school reforms, to job training rather than jobs.

Accordingly, such an analysis must include the present socio-economic status, values, hopes, and aspirations of Hispanic families, as well as their history and their interactions with the various institutions that influence and control them. We need to ask different types of questions: Why are schools and teachers failing to teach Hispanic youngsters? Why do the millions of dollars spent on job training fail to result in subsequent employment? Why are the churches, in some instances, not responding to Hispanic needs? Why are health, mental health, and related human service agencies similarly unresponsive? And why are Hispanics not receiving their fair share of the vast resources of our society, despite their contributions to national life and progress?

In order to assess the effects that health, mental health, and human services have on Hispanic families, one must consider three fundamental, interrelated issues: (1) the development of public policy on a "universal" basis; (2) the monolingual/monocultural nature of health, mental health, and human services planning and delivery; and (3) the economic status of the Hispanic population.

The "universal" approach to public or social policy (i.e., the design and implementation of programs to cover an entire population) negates the special needs and problems experienced by Hispanic families. This approach, for example, in failing to consider the short average life span of Mexican Americans (59.7 years) and Puerto Ricans, precludes many from ever benefiting from contributions to Social Security. It also leads to the exclusion of segments of the population that, for political and/or economic reasons, do not fit the criteria for eligibility. For instance, Mexican Americans and Puerto Ricans who comprised a large segment of the agricultural labor force through the 1960s were excluded from coverage under the Social Security Act. The nature of the problems confronting Hispanic families calls for the enactment of public policy on a "selective" basis. Health services for migrant and seasonal farmworkers, the Cuban Refugee Program, and bilingual/bicultural education are examples of programs enacted on a "selective" basis.

The provision of services based on a monolingual/monocultural framework, i.e., based on the English language and the dominant culture, is another concern related to the "universal" vs. "selective" issue just discussed. Although health, mental health, and human services, as a question of national policy, are to be provided to all without discrimination, Hispanic families are often excluded because their language and culture are left out and not accounted for in the planning, development, and delivery of these services. The lack of bilingual/bicultural professional staff, the location of services away from Hispanic *barrios* or neighborhoods, and the reluctance to develop services within an Hispanic cultural framework ultimately deny Hispanics access to health, mental health, and human service programs.

The need for health, mental health, and human services among Hispanic families is interrelated with their low economic or poverty status. Low income prevents them from maintaining healthy nutritional standards and denies them access to necessary, but costly health services. This is evident in high infant mortality rates, a shorter life span, learning problems faced by children in the school system, and other health and mental health problems which frequently become chronic.

Having considered the key issues, we must examine, in a critical manner, our place in the world. The dialectic of viewing ourselves in the context of the situation confronting us will lead us, as Octavio Paz has said, " . . . not only in knowing ourselves, but, as much or more, in freeing ourselves." The possibility of freedom that this activity unfolds is "an invitation to action."

The Hispanic population in the United States will double in the next 20 years and will constitute the largest ethnic minority in this country. The future prospects for this population remain dismal in light of the following factors:

- Mexican Americans and Puerto Ricans (who account for 71 percent of the Hispanic population) comprise the youngest population in the country (with a median age of about 18 years) and have one of the lowest levels of education.
- This low level of education relegates Hispanics to menial, low-paying jobs which result in conditions of poverty and familial stress with the concomitant problems of poor health, malnutrition, mental illness, delinquency, school dropouts, family breakdown, and other socio-economic ills that perpetuate the cycle of poverty.
- Present social policies at the National and State level continue to be predicated, for the most part, according to a "universal" perspective which precludes the development of "selective" policies and specialized programs designed to relate specifically to the particular needs, problems, and potentials of Hispanic families.

REFERENCES

Conde, Carlos (ed.). *A New Era: The Spanish Speaking People of the United States.* Washington, D.C.: the Cabinet Committee on Opportunities for the Spanish Speaking, 1970.

Grebler, Leo. Mexican immigration to the United States: the record and its implications. *Mexican American Study Project, Advance Report 2.* Los Angeles: University of California, 1965.

Hernandez, Luis. *A Forgotten American.* New York: Anti-Defamation League of B'nai B'rith, 1970.

Illinois State Advisory Committee, U.S. Commission on Civil Rights. Bilingual/bicultural education—a privilege or a right? May 1974. (Typed manuscript.)

Ramirez, Manuel and Castaneda, Alfredo. *Cultural Democracy, Bicognitive Development and Education.* New York: Academic Press, 1974.

U.S. Bureau of the Census. *Current Population Reports,* Series P-20, No. 213, "Persons of Spanish Origin in the United States: November 1969." Washington, D.C.: Government Printing Office, 1971.

THE VALUE OF A HUMANISTIC MODEL IN SERVING HISPANIC FAMILIES

Javier Saenz

Despite some progress in the last few years, members of Hispanic families tend to fare poorly in receiving social and human services in this country. The factors compounding this inequity are socio-economic disadvantage, cultural differences and conflicts, underutilization of services, and a lack of sufficient clinical and rehabilitation services designed and delivered by Hispanic professionals and paraprofessionals. This paper, based on my experience as both an Hispanic consumer and an Hispanic professional provider of human services, explores the reasons for the problems we face and highlights some of our progress in resolving them. It also describes a humanistic program model of human services designed by Hispanics to serve members of Hispanic families and the poor alike. This program—the Minority Human Service Training Program—was initiated and is promoted and maintained by the Salt Lake Spanish-Speaking Health and Mental Health Task Force in cooperation with the Granite Community Mental Health Center and the University of Utah in Salt Lake City.* (This effort is financially supported by a grant awarded to the Task Force by the National Institute of Mental Health.) Finally, this paper notes some implications of two recent laws—the 1975 amendments to the Community Mental Health Centers Act (P.L. 94-63) and the 1974 Health Planning and Resources Development Act (P.L. 93-641)—in effecting possible changes in the delivery of services to Hispanic families.

An Overview of Problems and Progress

When we speak of Hispanics, we are referring to this country's more than 11 million residents of "Spanish origin" who make the United States the fifth largest Spanish-speaking country in the world. Of the total number of Hispanics reporting in the Census Bureau's March 1976 Current Population Survey, about 6.6 million were of Mexican origin, 1.8 million of Puerto Rican origin, 700,000 of Cuban origin, 800,000 of Central or South American origin, and 1.3 million of "other" Spanish origin. These figures should be viewed as quite conservative estimates in light of the fact that the Census Bureau itself has acknowledged serious undercounts of the Hispanic population in past and current surveys (although some remedies are promised for the 1980 census). These estimates, it should be noted, do not include about 3.2 million persons living in Puerto Rico or

---

*The Task Force is an incorporated, nonprofit group of interested Spanish-speaking citizens concerned about improving health and mental health services in the Greater Salt Lake area. They represent community organizations, employees and employers in various service agencies, and consumers of services. The Task Force office is at 175 East 2100 South, Building 5, 3rd Floor, Salt Lake City 84115. Telephone: (801) 484-8713/14.

some six to 12 million Spanish-speaking undocumented aliens in the continental United States. In all, the Spanish-speaking represent the second largest ethnic/cultural minority in the country today.

Despite geographical and, in some cases, racial differences among Hispanic subgroups, all share certain cultural and socio-economic similarities. For a highly significant proportion of Hispanics, education and employment are critical problem areas. With regard to educational attainment for Hispanics age 35 and older, the highest level of education is 8.5 median years vs. 12 years for Anglos. Less than 12 percent of all Spanish-speaking adults have attended college. In a survey of selected mental health personnel, Ruiz (1971) identified 58 Hispanics among approximately 28,500 psychologists and 20 Hispanics among approximately 16,000 psychiatrists. Similar low proportions exist in most other professions in the fields of mental health and related human services (Olmedo and Lopez, 1977). In fact, only 25 percent of the Spanish-speaking are in white collar jobs compared to 41 percent of the rest of the population (Duran, 1975).

Many Hispanics lack the appropriate academic credentials and/or skills needed to secure employment and are affected adversely by rigid personnel and program requirements. They are disproportionately vulnerable to unemployment as well as to the stresses and conflicts related to financial disadvantage and the low social status of poverty. Incomes of the Spanish-speaking are 23.2 percent below the 1975 poverty level of approximately $5,000 annual income for a non-farm family of four, compared to 11.6 percent for all Americans; unemployment is high, 12.2 percent for the Spanish-speaking compared to 8.5 percent for all others (U.S. Department of Labor, 1975).

One of the more common conflicts prevalent among all minorities is caused by the discrepancy between the need for acceptance and the amount and quality of acceptance their environment is willing to grant them. Some minority group members may fall ill or "mentally ill" in order to secure the attention and concern they need and may not otherwise be able to obtain. In other words, through illness they may seek to justify the attention they need for existence and identity.

Hispanic families tend to come into conflict with the dominant society because their value system contrasts sharply with that of the majority and because no sustained effort has been made to adapt services to this basic difference and to consequent divergent needs. Let us review some of the components of this conflict in value systems. There is a significant minority of Hispanics who speak little or no English and recognize Spanish as their first language (Alvarez, 1975). They continue to base family structure on respect for parental authority, not on the kind of egalitarianism between parents and offspring that is often prevalent in the dominant society. More often than not, ties between relatives are strong and run deep, and closeness and interdependency are encouraged in contrast to the sense of independence or autonomy that most members of the dominant society seek to achieve. The old are venerated, not discarded as being of little or no value, and are usually provided for in the home, not in nursing homes. Discipline is maintained more by mercy and compassion than by rules and punitive measures. An attitude of concern toward others is far more common than an attitude of "minding one's own business." Pride in one's achievements is a unique heritage and value of Hispanics in contrast to the attitudes of disinterest, non-involvement, and depersonalization that often characterize the performance of others in our society. Hispanics as a group are, in effect, a "natural" for a humanistic model of service—a model based on accounting for individual differences, providing services in accord with individual needs, and promoting each person's uniqueness and betterment within his or her own values and reality conditions.

Most mental health centers, drug abuse and alcohol programs, and other social and rehabilitation services tend to be perceived by Hispanics as designed to deliver impersonal services that are ineffective in reaching the needs and life styles of Hispanic families. As Torrey (1968) illustrates:

> Psychiatric services in the United States are sharply bound by both class and cultural values . . . the vast majority of services, delivered by highly trained professionals stressing insight and autonomy, evolved to meet the needs of upper-class America and are vaguely assumed to emanate from God-given principles. The resulting lack of class and cultural perspective produces services for minority groups that, when they exist at all, are both illogical and irrelevant . . . No real effort has been made to conceptualize logical and relevant psychiatric services for them. They must make do with what services are available as decreed by the majority culture and majority class.

Of some 800 mental health centers in this country, approximately 40, plus a handful of programs in alcohol abuse and drug rehabilitation, are merging traditional therapeutic techniques with humanistic planning and service delivery designed to respect the cultural identity of the consumer and to recognize and maintain the individuality of the Hispanic. Considering socio-economic differences and cultural conflicts, it is not difficult to understand why Hispanics are underrepresented as staff and workers in mental health and human services. It is also quite obvious why Hispanics underutilize these service delivery systems.

Within the culture of this country an individual is perceived as mentally healthy when he or she is capable of adapting to his or her life conditions, when he or she has the ability to resolve problems by assuming the values of the dominant society. But when an individual's adaptions differ from the values of the majority, that person is seen as deviant, mentally disturbed, delinquent, or criminal and, more often than not, is punished, not treated. I do not intend to imply that severe mental illness, appropriately diagnosed, does not exist; when an appropriate diagnosis is made with an understanding of Hispanic culture and mores, it is unquestionable that some of the traditional medical modalities of treatment are effective in assisting Hispanic family members. But a cultural understanding of such persons must accompany the use and application of medical, psychological, and social skills (Torrey, 1970).

Professionals from the dominant culture who plan and direct the provision of most rehabilitation, clinical, and other mental health services complain often that such services are underutilized by Hispanic families. They have gone so far as to assert that the reason for this phenomenon is that Hispanics prefer folk medicine or faith healers (Lubchansky, Ergi, and Stokes, 1970; Garrison, 1971 and 1972). Recent studies have proved otherwise, i.e., when efficient and "acculturated" professional treatment practices are offered to Hispanics, these (and not substitutes) are fully utilized (Alvarez, 1975).

11

Service providers also allege that they are not fully utilized because Hispanics are "not ready" for their services or because Hispanics are "better prepared" to tolerate stress than are members of the majority culture. Unfortunately, these rationalizations tend to originate not from evidence, but from a lack of interest on the part of the therapist toward Hispanic consumers, a lack of interest based on little or no understanding of their problems and cultural adaptations.

Hispanic consumers tend to be intimidated by the business-like atmosphere of clinical services. They see the service professional as impersonal and uninvolved, less concerned about listening to their specific problems as they perceive and feel them and more concerned about fitting such problems into his or her professional and personal priorities. Hispanic consumers tend to prefer a therapist who is active as a helping partner, willing to assist and offer advice when necessary.

A brief look at the various stages of development of human service systems in this country reveals a clear lack of awareness of cultural differences and socio-economic problems relevant to planning and implementing effective services to Hispanics, especially to Hispanic drug and alcohol abusers. As a result, we continue to seek out more relevant and effective services. In this regard, some progress has been made and new programs have emerged. In 1972 the National Institute of Mental Health (NIMH) held a series of planning meetings in New York City, the purpose of which was to determine needs and relevant services to the Spanish-speaking. Three areas of need were identified: research, training, and direct services. In addition, NIMH reorganized its structure and staffing patterns to include representation by Hispanics as well as other minorities. What has emerged as a result?

With regard to research, three organizations have developed with differing emphases but complementary purposes and activities: COSSMHO—The National Coalition of Hispanic Mental Health and Human Services Organizations which, through its National Office in Washington, D.C., and its nationwide network of member agencies and individuals, acts as a force to sustain the ongoing identification of present and newly emerging needs and to generate solutions within and among Hispanic communities, as well as collaborative efforts between Hispanics and non-Hispanics; and two Hispanic research centers—the Spanish-Speaking Mental Health Research Center at the University of California, Los Angeles, and the Hispanic Research Center at Fordham University in New York City—which promote efforts by Hispanic scholars to develop knowledge on which to base and design better research and service programs for Hispanics. These organizations receive grant support for project activities from the NIMH Center for Minority Group Mental Health Programs.

The Center also promotes training through the Minority Fellowship Program which makes funds available to selected national professional societies for use in granting fellowships to members of ethnic minority groups interested in pursuing careers in the behavioral sciences. In this regard, awards for training researchers have been made to the American Psychiatric Association, the American Psychological Association, the American Sociological Association, the American Nurses' Association, and the Council on Social Work Education. Moreover, these organizations have had applications approved to expand their efforts to include the training of ethnic minority Ph.D. candidates in clinical services. The

Center also has encouraged scientific writing, public administration, and other professional training.

There have been some beginning efforts to promote credentialing and recognition of the special skills of former drug and alcohol abusers as counselors and of paraprofessionals as legitimate workers in human service fields. Recognition of this latter group has been long overdue—it is well known that many paraprofessionals have contributed much to improving the knowledge and skills of professionals in various aspects of the delivery of services, especially in the areas of rehabilitation, drug abuse, and alcoholism. Although they have demonstrated, beyond question, their abilities to reach out to consumers and serve them with dedication and skill, paraprofessionals have often been excluded from better jobs due to overly rigid program and personnel requirements.

A number of programs have emerged to provide services to Hispanic family members—for example, partial hospitalization services such as those developed at the Los Angeles Rest Haven Hospital and mental health services such as those developed at *La Frontera* in Tucson, *Servicios de la Raza* in Denver, *Aliviane* in El Paso, the Community Mental Health Center in East Los Angeles, *La Clinica Hispana* in New Haven, *El Centro de la Causa* in westside Chicago, and the Minority Human Service Training Program in Salt Lake City, to name only a few. These programs represent various humanistic models of providing services to Hispanics. Paradoxically, these successful programs are often under severe economic pressures, as well as excessive administrative and professional scrutiny, and are accorded only marginal acceptance and recognition outside Hispanic circles despite their record of meeting the needs of our communities.

A Look at a Humanistic Model of Services Delivery

Drawing on my own professional experience, let me now describe the humanistic model of services delivery that was designed and is promoted by Hispanics to serve their community in the Salt Lake City area. The purpose of this program—the Minority Human Service Training Program—is to serve and train people from Spanish-speaking backgrounds, as well as other minority and disadvantaged groups, in mental health and human services. Trainees provide services while at the same time they achieve a two-year Associate of Arts degree from the College of Social and Behavioral Sciences of the University of Utah. They acquire 95 university credit hours—this enables them to continue with their education if they so desire. Trainees become competent practitioners in working with their own people, in their own language, in their own neighborhoods. They are trained in interviewing techniques, crisis intervention, and family and group counseling, all of which originate from learning how to formulate a case and establish a plan of action.* They learn how to provide a variety of social services—from helping persons apply for and obtain public assistance, Social Security benefits, or Food Stamps to counseling persons in the clinic, at home or at work, or in whatever setting is

---

*This process facilitates organization of information, promotes efficiency in treatment planning, and results in a concise description of an individual and situation. It is based on Dr. Norman Anderson's conceptualization of patient formulations and is adapted for use in the Adult Day Care Unit of the Granite Community Mental Health Center, Salt Lake City.

appropriate to the consumer's needs, given his or her life style, problems, and concerns.

The number of trainees in the program is kept to a minimum (25) in order to maintain a demand for such workers and not generate an oversupply. Job descriptions and a career ladder have been developed for the program and are utilized by the Salt Lake County Merit System.

The Adult Day Care Center, which is a unit of service of the Granite Community Mental Health Center, has been designed and developed to provide rich and humane experiences for both trainees and consumers. The unit is composed of three service areas—the day treatment program, the aftercare program, and the outreach program.

The day treatment program provides services, eight hours a day, three days a week, to individuals age 18 and older who are functioning well enough in the community not to require 24-hour hospitalization, but who need more than traditional outpatient support. Services include group counseling, activity therapy, family and individual counseling, conjoint therapy, and crisis intervention. Available in this program are evening groups for individuals, marriage counseling, and education and information classes for the community.

The aftercare program provides follow-up services to individuals placed in nursing homes who are identified as psychiatric patients. Services include consultation services to nursing home management staff, the conduct of re-socialization/remotivation groups, and medical re-evaluation of medications. The program offers, when appropriate, a weekly social group for nursing home patients and for isolated persons in the community who are former State hospital patients but do not benefit from traditional therapy. This aspect of the program caters to the older citizen and to those who live alone without benefit of social contacts.

The outreach program extends services to those community residents who have been unable to utilize traditional services provided by mental health centers due to language barriers, cultural differences, lack of transportation, and/or lack of information. This program serves a population of all ages (with mild to severe personal and social problems) in their own language and in their own homes when necessary. The range of service offered is from acting as an advocate or educator to being a therapist or friend.

Throughout their training program, trainees undergo an intense, thorough exposure to a broad range of traditional counseling techniques and principles which are adapted to a humanistic treatment model. They are adequately prepared to work in most human service agencies after training is completed.

In summary, the Minority Human Service Training Program combines recognition of the needs of Hispanic consumers and the poor with the provision of services especially designed to meet their needs. It also brings together the efforts of a community mental health center, a university, and the Spanish-speaking community. This review of such a humanistic model of services delivery and training leads us to a further consideration of future program approaches most suitable for aiding Hispanic families.

Opportunities Provided in Recent Legislation

Some beginning efforts by the Federal Government to implement and support health and mental health programs with potential to benefit Hispanic consumers have been cited in the introduction to this paper. It is imperative, therefore, to discuss here the most significant changes that may arise in health and mental health services delivery as a result of two recent laws—the 1974 Health Planning and Resources Development Act (P.L. 93-641) and the 1975 amendments to the Community Mental Health Centers Act (P.L. 94-63). These laws attempt to offset or overcome problems arising from the proliferation and fragmentation of programs and to make these programs more in touch with the needs of local communities.

The first of these laws establishes a nationwide network of local health planning bodies, known as health systems agencies (HSAs), which are responsible for planning, developing, and implementing the delivery of various health and health-related services, including those for the mentally and emotionally handicapped. They also have authority to review and recommend uses for several billion dollars in Federal funds made available for services and facilities under several statutory authorities—the Community Mental Health Centers Act, the Alcoholism Treatment Act, and the Public Health Service Act. These HSAs are our direct avenue for input in the development, as well as the improvement, of health and health-related services in our communities.

The second of these laws expands the number and types of services that community mental health centers must provide. These now include emergency services, outpatient services, consultation and education, screening of residents for referral to State mental health facilities and treatment if appropriate, follow-up care for persons discharged from inpatient services, specialized services for children and the elderly, transitional halfway house services for the mentally ill to obviate the need for hospitalization, programs for drug and alcohol abuse treatment and prevention, and inpatient, day care, and partial hospitalization services. Agencies and centers must provide services that "reach out" to those who would not otherwise utilize their services. And, in areas with substantial numbers of persons of "limited English-speaking ability," all services must be made available in the bilingual/bicultural context appropriate to the person(s) being served.

The analysis and interpretation of these laws introduce guidelines for health, mental health, and human services that affect primarily the poor, among whom are many Hispanic families. It is mandated, for example, that those receiving services should have sufficient input in the planning of these services through their local HSAs. Professionals may assist in the design of programs, but only in partnership with those whom they serve. Likewise, follow-up care, as provided by nursing homes and boarding homes, must be redefined in terms of serving the long-term consumer, the poor, and the elderly, and in terms of providing more humane and comprehensive services.

It is known that because of socio-economic status, culture, and life style, Spanish-speaking family members are most likely to respond to programs that reach out to them in the familiar atmosphere of their own homes and neighborhoods. These services, properly staffed and supported, would be a welcome addition offering great potential for assisting

Hispanics. Drug and alcohol abuse programs utilizing Hispanic professionals and paraprofessionals to provide culture-specific services to their afflicted peers would also be welcomed.

Despite these promising possibilities, the laws still present us with a familiar handicap. I am referring to the procedure of dispersing Federal funds through State and local governments. Although this procedure is logical in theory, the result has often been neglect of minority needs due to regional and local prejudices and pressures. Nevertheless, these laws can be utilized as a basis for fashioning the development of more humanistic models of services delivery, models which can be designed in accord with the specific needs and concerns of Hispanic families and the poor. Making this hope a reality is the challenge confronting Hispanic professionals and paraprofessionals in human service fields as well as our partners in government and voluntary agencies.

REFERENCES

Alvarez, Rodolfo (ed.). *Delivery of Services for Latino Community Mental Health.* Monograph No. 2. Los Angeles: University of California, Spanish-Speaking Mental Health Research and Development Program, 1975.

Duran, Ruben (ed.). *Salubridad Chicana: Su Preservación y Mantenimiento—The Chicano Plan for Mental Health.* Boulder, Colorado: Western Interstate Commission for Higher Education (WICHE), 1975.

Garrison, Vivian. Social networks and social change in the 'culture of poverty.' Paper presented at the 138th annual meeting of the American Association for the Advancement of Science, Philadelphia, Pennsylvania, December 1971.

_____ . *Espiritismo:* implications for provision of mental health services to Puerto Rican populations. Paper presented at the 8th annual meeting of the Southern Anthropological Society, Columbus, Missouri, February 24-26, 1972.

Lubchansky, Isaac; Ergi, Gladys; and Stokes, Janet. Puerto Rican spiritualists view mental illness: the faith healer as a paraprofessional. *American Journal of Psychiatry,* 1970, *127,* 3, 312-21.

Olmedo, Esteban, and Lopez, Steven (eds.). *Hispanic Mental Health Professionals.* Monograph No. 5. Los Angeles: University of California, Spanish-Speaking Mental Health Research Center, 1977.

Ruiz, R.A. Relative frequency of Americans with Spanish surnames in associations of psychology, psychiatry, and sociology. *American Psychologist,* 1971, *26,* 11, 1022-24.

Torrey, E. Fuller. Psychiatric services for Mexican Americans. Unpublished manuscript, 1968.

_____ . The irrelevancy of traditional mental health services for urban Mexican Americans. Paper presented at the meeting of the American Orthopsychiatry Association, San Francisco, California, March 1970.

U.S. Bureau of the Census. *Current Population Reports,* Series P-20, No. 302, "Persons of Spanish Origin in the United States: March 1976." Washington, D.C.: Government Printing Office, 1976.

U.S. Department of Labor, Bureau of Labor Statistics. *Employment and Earnings,* 1975, *22,* 7, 159.

OTHER SOURCES

Boucher, S.W. (ed.). Mexican American mental health issues: present realities and future strategies. Paper presented at the Western Interstate Commission for Higher Education conference, Goleta, California, June 10-12, 1970.

Cabinet Committee on Opportunities for the Spanish-Speaking. *Annual Report, Fiscal Year 1971.* Washington, D.C.: Government Printing Office, 1972.

Curren, D.J. (ed.). Legislative notes: major health planning law enacted. *COSSMHO Reporter,* 1975, *1,* 3, April-May, 1.

Curren, D.J.; Rivera, J. Julian; and Sanchez, R.B. (eds.). *Proceedings of Puerto Rican Conferences on Human Services.* Washington, D.C.: COSSMHO—The National Coalition of Hispanic Mental Health and Human Services Organizations, 1975.

Latino Task Force on Community Mental Health Training. *Latino Community Mental Health.* Monograph No. 1. Los Angeles: University of California, Spanish-Speaking Mental Health Research and Development Program, 1974.

Quervalu, Ivan. Cultural factors and mental health issues: a Puerto Rican perspective. *COSSMHO Reporter,* 1975, *2,* 1, January, 1.

Saenz, Javier. Mental health movement in Utah: a study of change in mental health. Doctoral dissertation, School of Social and Behavioral Sciences, Social Psychology Department, University of Utah, Salt Lake City, 1974.

Sanchez, R.B. National legislation and Latino mental health: the impact of history on mental health and ways specific laws can improve service delivery to Hispanos. Paper presented at the annual meeting of the National Council of Community Mental Health Centers, Denver, Colorado, February 22-25, 1976. Available from COSSMHO—The National Coalition of Hispanic Mental Health and Human Services Organizations, 1725 K St., N.W., Suite 1212, Washington, D.C. 20006.

U.S. Bureau of the Census. *Current Population Reports,* Series P-60, No. 102, "Consumer Income, 1976." Washington, D.C.: Government Printing Office, 1976.

Weinburg, S.K. (ed.). *The Sociology of Mental Disorders: Analyses and Readings in Psychiatric Sociology.* Chicago: Aldine Publishing Company, 1967.

CHICANOS IN THE UNITED STATES:
An Overview of Socio-Historical Context and Emerging Perspectives
Miguel Montiel

Ortega y Gasset, the great Spanish philosopher, once said that man does not generally live his genuine life but rather a life defined by others in society. This circumstance leads to a state of crisis which he defined as "the transition which a man makes from a life attached to some things and supported by them to a life attached to another and supported by other things" (Ortega y Gasset, 1957). Chicanos or Mexican Americans or Mexicans in the United States are facing a crisis, for those things which they believe and are attached to have been continuously under attack. Their history, body of knowledge, and strategies designed to integrate them into the dominant society have, in the words of the Chicano philosopher Tomas Atencio (1972), "been derived from someone else's action." The attacks against their culture and language, the neglect and distortion of their history, the rejection and alienation from their mother country, and the external definitions of their existence must provide the perspective for understanding the Chicano in this country.

This paper presents a socio-historical overview of the current status of Chicanos in the United States. It begins with an analysis of the negative manner in which the social sciences have defined the Chicano. It is followed by a brief history of Chicanos in this country, beginning with the conquest of the borderlands and continuing up through the ebb and flow of immigration—legal and "illegal"—since the Mexican Revolution of 1910. It was during these times of the struggle for survival and the search for a better life that *barrios* evolved in U.S. metropolitan areas. Although most of their settlements were in the Southwest, Mexicans settled as far away as Kansas City, St. Louis, and Chicago. The development of the *barrios* and the role of the Catholic Church constitute the third and fourth parts of this paper. It is in the context of the external definitions and of the history of Chicano-Anglo relations that the objective status of Chicanos is presented. The fifth section of this paper is an analysis that includes population breakdown, family, income, education, health, and other key demographic characteristics. The final section briefly identifies some of the major Chicano academic perspectives that have emerged.

The "Sick" Minorities

It would not be an exaggeration to state that the medical model, in one form or another, has dominated the study of Chicanos in the United States. This model originated in biology and postulates that there can be

Author's note. Part of the data for this paper was collected and analyzed under a grant sponsored by the Ford Foundation.

no cure without discovering the etiology of maladaptive behavior. Deficit, deprivation, and disadvantage are common adjectives used in the research enterprise to describe racial and ethnic minorities. These adjectives indicate that there is something missing in the development of the individual. The pathology model is essentially a medical model. David Matza, a Berkeley sociologist, in discussing much of the research on deviation (1969), states that its purpose "has been to assist established society ultimately to rid itself of such troublesome activities." Research on Chicanos has followed a similar course. Several examples illustrate this most important point.

1. The "culture of poverty" negates the essence of the anthropological notions of culture and stresses the highly negative approaches and values that are thought to be distinctive of the lower class poor, such as a disorganized family structure, violence, present time orientation, illegitimacy, and numerous other "internal causes" (Valentine, 1968).

2. The research on early childhood education maintains that minority children are unable to learn in the schools because of inadequate mothering and an environment that does not provide adequate sensory stimulation for cognitive growth (Baratz and Baratz, 1970).

3. The psychoanalytically-oriented psychologists, led by David Mc-Clelland, maintain that poor people lack achievement motivation and, consequently, academic, social, and economic achievement because of the inability of the culture to develop necessary attitudes such as future time orientation, stress on individual achievement, and a sense of control over one's destiny.

The common element in these examples is the stress on etiology and the assumption that the causes for the deviance are inside the person, the family, or the culture under study.* Thus, Grebler (in Grebler, Moore, and Guzman, 1970), begins his description of the Mexican American family by citing Moynihan who explained the low status of black people in terms of an "unmotivated" male personality resulting from the "traditional matricentric family." Both families, according to Grebler, basically produce the "same kind of young man—one who drops out of school because he is preoccupied with immediate pleasure." The social science literature which stresses notions of deficit, deprivation, and disadvantage implies that something is missing inside these people and that this should be corrected. Correction, according to Matza (1969), "reflects the easily appreciated social view that persons who have strayed from moral standards ought to be persuaded by a variety of means to return to the

---

*Valentine (1968) mentions numerous methodological weaknesses in many studies that have dealt with minorities and lower income persons. It is evident from the many research sources that there is an obvious bias for data that portray pathology. Police, court, and social work reports generally focus on behavior that, by its very nature, is corrective. Also, census data that are used to identify "disorganized" families (by which is meant female-headed households) do not *per se* document the absence of males in these households. Witness the great number of "living together" arrangements among middle class and upper class persons that do not fall into this pathological interpretation. One statistical description can be interpreted in several different ways.

According to Valentine, the research of Oscar Lewis provides a good example of these methodological weaknesses. Lewis relied on social workers to find an appropriate family for study. How can he claim, asks Valentine, that this family is representative of the community from which it was selected? In addition, Valentine says, the interpretations do not follow from the data. For example, Lewis states that disorganization and a narrow perspective are characteristic of the "culture of poverty," yet Valentine finds a highly organized community with churches, stores, and bars that are centers of interaction.

fold, and it argues that knowledge may be put to that service."

Let me briefly point out how such notions about Chicanos might be applied by social workers, educators, and others working with Chicano families. The following traits, for example, are found in the literature as explanations for the so-called "failure" of Chicano youngsters in school: families indulge male children, thus hampering "need achievement"; lack independence training; have lax habits; do not stress education; are present time oriented; speak Spanish; think too much of their own misfortune; and, overall, hamper acculturation and assimilation (Clark, 1959; Madsen, 1964; Manuel, 1965; Hayden, 1966; Heller, 1966). It follows that if these are the forces impinging on the "proper" socialization process of Chicanos, they must be removed and be replaced by socialization traits exhibited by individuals and families who have been defined as "successful." Inevitably, the ideal individual or family type is patterned on the social worker, the educator, and others relying on their interpretations in working with Chicano families.

These views of cultural inferiority are reflected by a mother who described her experience with the school system upon her arrival from Mexico. "In the early days, school officials did not allow children to speak Spanish. Those who did were punished. My second child would rush out of the classroom at break time and urinate on the school patio because he didn't know how to ask to be excused." Although such extreme situations no longer occur, the memory of them and the negative attitudes of school officials still linger.

The idea of cultural inferiority and the "uplift" strategy, implied in the literature and in the actions of many school and government officials, according to Miller (1969), ignores the issue of self-determination. "It is absurd," he argues, "to apply the label of psychological damage to a people as one would to a person." Ethnic self-determination, he continues, "takes its operational form from an ideology of cultural pluralism. To the extent that this ideology is subverted, to that extent it is an evil enterprise."

In sum, the literature, in focusing on the "deficits" of Chicanos, points to what is alleged to be wrong with them and insists that they be transformed in accord with an ambiguous, undefined "success" or "middle class" model. What is *not* ambiguous, however, is the notion that what exists in the Chicano community is inadequate and inferior. It is this corrective framework that has prevented social scientists from accurately depicting the experiences of Chicano families.

Journey to the North

Most Chicanos, like Anglos of European origin, share the experience of ancestral or recent migration from their homeland to the United States. Unlike them, however, the section of this country where most Mexican immigrants first settled once belonged to Mexico.* "Manifest destiny" and

---

*This historical fact has led numerous Chicano scholars to argue that the Southwest is a conquered entity and that Chicanos are a colonized people. Although, at face value, the argument is attractive, the evidence points elsewhere. The logic of interpreting the present Chicano situation in terms of this historical precedent falls apart when it is realized that there were only about 100,000 Mexicans in the Southwest at the time of the annexation. There are now as many as eight to nine million Mexican Americans in this country, most of whom are immigrants or sons and daughters of immigrants. The key question is whether these millions cling to the notion that the Southwest belongs to them and that they migrated north with the idea that it is, in fact, their country. An exception to this generalization exists in northern New Mexico and parts of Texas where the residents clearly trace their lineage in the area prior to the 1846-1848 War with Mexico.

the political instability in Mexico in the middle of the 19th century led to what we now call the Southwest.

The Mexicans living in this region at the time of the Treaty of Guadalupe-Hidalgo, the surrender settlement between the United States and Mexico, were given the option of staying on their lands and becoming U.S. citizens or leaving their lands and migrating south of the new U.S.-Mexican border. It is estimated that about 100,000 Mexicans lived in the Southwest at the time (Saunders, 1950). Clearly, a historical paradox exists. On the one hand, Mexicans constitute a population "native" to the Southwest and, on the other, they are the most recent immigrants in this "nation of immigrants."* The small handful of Mexicans in the Southwest at the time of the War with Mexico is greatly overshadowed by the tremendous influx of immigrants from Mexico during this century.

It was not until around 1918, following the period of social and political change ushered in by the Mexican Revolution of 1910, that the first great flow of Mexican immigrants began. The migration continued unabated for well over a decade until it was drastically curtailed at the time of the Great Depression. The Mexican Revolution, the demand for labor during World War I, and the prosperity of the 1920s were all important factors in opening up the U.S.-Mexican border. During the Depression, the U.S. Government tightened its surveillance of illegal entrants, restricted the number of legal entrants, and sanctioned the massive deportation of Mexicans from this country.

The labor demand created by World War II and the subsequent expansion of agribusiness created the next great influx of Mexican immigrants, with the greatest number coming during the 1950s. This influx ended in 1964 with the termination of the *bracero* program. Mexicans have continued to migrate here, legally and otherwise. The numbers fluctuate depending on union pressure, variation in technology and automation, the need for unskilled labor, welfare policies, and, most significantly, the economic conditions in Mexico and the United States.

The movements which these social and economic events triggered were massive. Here are some estimates regarding Mexican immigrants legally admitted for permanent residence. As a response to the upheavals of the Mexican Revolution, approximately 200,000 crossed the border. From 1920 to 1929, about 490,000 settled here, primarily in response to the aftermath of World War I, the increased need for cheap labor in the developing Southwest, and the after effects of the Mexican Revolution. The decade of the Depression saw only a small increase—28,000 immigrants. The years from 1940 to 1949 saw a modest increase of 54,000. The 1950-1959 period attracted nearly 300,000; the 1960-1964 period, a total of 217,827. From 1960 until 1968, there was a steady flow slightly above 40,000 per year (Samora, 1971). Table I presents a detailed breakdown of the flow of Mexican migration to this country from 1900 to 1973.

---

*The American Indians are the only natives of this land. This fact adds further difficulty to the "colonization" interpretation. It should be noted, however, that Chicanos are a hybrid people and that biologically, culturally, and philosophically, it is possible to trace their lineage to Native Americans. The argument presented here is not to negate these roots but simply to state that most Mexicans, since the Mexican Revolution of 1910, have entered a country that is philosophically and politically controlled by Anglo-Saxon laws. To this extent, they entered an alien country. However, the linkages between Chicanos and Native Americans merit extensive discussion.

TABLE I
NUMBER OF MEXICAN IMMIGRANTS
COMPARED WITH ALL U.S. IMMIGRANTS
1900-1973a

Periodb	Mexicanc	Total	Mexican as Percent of Total
1900-1904	2,259	3,255,149	.07
1905-1909	21,732	4,947,239	.44
1910-1914	82,588	5,174,701	1.60
1915-1919	91,075	1,172,679	7.77
1920-1924	249,248	2,774,600	8.98
1925-1929	238,527	1,520,910	15.68
1930-1934	19,200	426,953	4.50
1935-1939	8,737	272,422	3.21
1940-1944	16,548	203,589	8.13
1945-1949	37,742	653,019	5.78
1950-1954	78,723	1,099,035	7.16
1955-1959	214,746	1,400,233	15.34
1960-1964	217,827	1,419,013	15.35
Annual Figures			
1965	37,969	296,697	12.79
1966	45,163	323,040	13.98
1967	42,371	361,972	11.71
1968	43,563	454,448	9.59
1969	44,623	358,579	12.44
1970	44,469	373,226	12.00
1971	50,103	360,478	13.89
1972	31,588	204,970	15.41
1973	64,865	154,882	41.88

SOURCES: Annual Reports of the U.S. Immigration and Naturalization Service and its predecessor agencies.

aReported figures for earlier periods should be considered approximations. All refer to persons legally admitted for permanent residence.

bFiscal years.

cClassified by country of birth, except for the periods 1935-1939 and 1940-1944 in which data refer to Mexico as the country of last permanent residence. Classifications reported indicate that numerical differences are relatively small. The "country of birth" classification was adopted here as the basic one, not only because it is definitionally superior, but also because characteristics of immigrants are reported on this basis.

The figures for entry of temporary Mexican workers are even more impressive. The *bracero* program, begun in 1942 as an emergency war measure designed to benefit the employer, subsidized by the U.S. Government, and operated for over 20 years thereafter, imported a total of

5.2 million *braceros*—4.8 million of whom entered the United States between 1951 and 1964, well after the war. Table II provides a breakdown of the number of *braceros* admitted from 1942 to 1967. What is even more astonishing is that, during the same period, over five million Mexican illegal aliens were apprehended by U.S. authorities (Samora, 1971).

For more than a half century, the question of illegal or undocumented aliens has been a perplexing problem for both the United States and Mexico. (Table III presents a breakdown of the number of such aliens reported from 1924 to 1973.) During times of economic prosperity, when there has been great need for inexpensive Mexican labor, the United States has encouraged both legal and illegal entry. However, economic setbacks immediately have resulted in retaliation and repatriation of illegal aliens. There have been three major periods during this brief history where the cycle has been clearly evident. During the Depression of the 1930s, in an effort to reduce the welfare rolls, it is estimated that more than 400,000 Mexicans, many of whom were American citizens, were repatriated, "sometimes on special trains subsidized by State and local governments" (Daniels, 1974). "Operation Wetback" in 1954 was the second period, with at least one million Mexicans being repatriated. This came on the heels of a similar effort in 1953 which saw well over 800,000 Mexican illegal aliens deported. In the 1970s we are again witnessing a similar effort on the part of the U.S. Government. Illegal or undocumented aliens are "blamed for taking jobs from American citizens, not paying taxes, and being a burden on our public welfare system" (Ramirez *et al.*, 1977). These attitudes do not seem to be supported by the evidence. Ramirez cites a study by Litton and Company:

> This study numbered 750 undocumented immigrants of whom 61 percent were Mexicans who worked in the Southwest. They earned, on the average, $1.71 per hour, far below the minimum wage and clearly not in competition with the average American worker. The study showed that 77 percent of the group had Federal income taxes withheld. It also showed that only 0.5 percent received welfare and less than 1.5 percent received Food Stamps.

Ramirez identifies "blaming the victim" as an unwritten, but recognized social policy: "In time of economic stress, that portion of the population that seems to be undesirable is scapegoated and blamed for economic problems."

The Barrio

Before the arrival of Anglo settlers in the borderlands, primarily in Texas and New Mexico, following the War of 1846-1848, there were Mexican settlements long in place. Even to this day, many retain the flavor of agrarian villages in northern Mexico. It is interesting to note that the language resembles the vocabulary and voice intonations of the *hombre de rancho*. However, most of the immigrants from Mexico in this century did not settle in these communities in northern New Mexico and southern Texas. The formation of the *barrios* in large U.S. metropolitan areas occurred because of the labor shortage created by both World Wars and the commensurate demand for cheap labor on the part of agricultural and mining interests in the expanding Southwest. The practice of recruiting

TABLE II
NUMBER AND ANNUAL AVERAGE EMPLOYMENT OF MEXICAN CONTRACT WORKERS ADMITTED FOR TEMPORARY WORK IN U.S. AGRICULTURE
1942-1967

Calendar Year	Number Admitted	Annual Average Employment*
1942	4,203	1,300
1943	52,098	15,600
1944	62,170	18,600
1945	49,454	14,800
1946	32,043	9,600
1947	19,632	5,900
1948	35,345	10,600
1949	107,000	32,100
1950	67,500	20,200
1951	192,000	57,600
1952	197,100	59,100
1953	201,380	70,700
1954	309,033	85,300
1955	398,650	112,800
1956	445,197	125,700
1957	436,049	132,200
1958	432,857	131,800
1959	437,643	135,900
1960	315,846	113,200
1961	291,420	95,700
1962	194,978	59,700
1963	186,865	45,900
1964	177,736	42,300
1965	20,284	2,200
1966	8,647	1,000
1967	6,125	600

SOURCES: Numbers of *braceros* and others admitted, as reported by the U.S. Department of Agriculture for 1942-1947 and thereafter by the Bureau of Employment Security, U.S. Department of Labor. Figures vary from those reported by the Immigration and Naturalization Service, partly because figures of the latter are for fiscal years. Data of the U.S. Department of Labor are used here because they have been converted by the Bureau of Employment Security to annual average employment for the period 1953-1967. See: House Committee on the Judiciary, *Study of Population and Immigration Problems,* Special Series No. 11 (1963), Appendix for Part II, Table 3, and current reports, *Farm Labor Developments,* by the Department of Labor. For years before 1953, above data on annual average employment are estimates constructed as follows. The above source shows the annual average employment of temporary Mexican workers in agriculture in the 1953-1962 period to equal 30.1 percent of the number of workers admitted. A ratio of 30 percent was applied to the years prior to 1953. This procedure assumes a constant relationship between admissions and duration of employment.

*Total man-months for the year divided by 12. Figures are rounded.

TABLE III
MEXICAN UNDOCUMENTED ALIENS REPORTED
1924-1973

YEAR	TOTAL	YEAR	TOTAL	YEAR	TOTAL
1924	4,614	1939	9,376	1954	1,075,168
1925	2,961	1940	8,051	1955	242,608
1926	4,047	1941	6,082	1956	72,442
1927	4,495	1942	DNA*	1957	44,451
1928	5,529	1943	8,189	1958	37,242
1929	8,538	1944	26,689	1959	30,196
1930	18,319	1945	63,602	1960	29,651
1931	8,409	1946	91,456	1961	29,817
1932	7,116	1947	182,986	1962	30,272
1933	15,875	1948	179,385	1963	39,124
1934	8,910	1949	278,538	1964	43,844
1935	9,139	1950	458,215	1965	55,349
1936	9,534	1951	500,000	1966	89,751
1937	9,535	1952	543,538	1967	108,327
1938	8,684	1953	865,318	1968	151,705
				1969	201,636
				1970	373,326
				1971	370,478
				1972	384,685
				1973	400,063

*Data not available

SOURCES: 1924-1941, Annual Reports of the Secretary of Labor. 1943-1960, special compilations of the Immigration and Naturalization Service. 1961-1973, Annual Reports of the Immigration and Naturalization Service.

NOTE: Until 1941 the Immigration and Naturalization Service (INS) was in the U.S. Department of Labor; since then, it has been in the U.S. Department of Justice. Over the years a variety of categories have been used to report Mexican undocumented aliens with some inconsistency. This table reflects those inconsistencies. Aliens Deported is a category that is consistently used for reporting Mexican undocumented aliens but does not include all Mexican undocumented aliens apprehended. It refers to those forcefully expelled from this country under warrant procedures. Mention is made of illegal entrants who are not allowed to remain. These are reported as departing without the benefit of deportation warrant procedures after showing their willingness to depart. The following categories have also been used: Aliens Debarred from Entry (Annual Report of the Commissioner-General of Immigration, 1924: 12-13, 125-29); Voluntary Removals (Annual Report of the Secretary of Labor, 1931: 53-55); Voluntary Departures (Annual Report of the Secretary of Labor, 1932: 73); Forced Departures without Deportation Warrants (Annual Report of the Secretary of Labor, 1939: 97; 1940: 110). The figures for the 1943-1960 period were furnished by the INS under Mexican Illegal Aliens Apprehended (this includes Deportations and Voluntary Departures). The figures for 1961-1969 are taken from the annual reports of those years under the category Deportable Aliens Found and/or Located. Even within the same report there are inconsistencies. In 1963, for example, on the same page, two figures are presented for Deportable Mexican Aliens: one is 38,866; the other, 39,124 (Annual Report of the INS, 1964: 8).

and contracting for labor in Mexico, or *rengances*, became a sophisticated method of exploitation and abuse that continues to this day. Many pioneering and now prominent American families still profit from this practice.

Historically, Mexican immigrants have been subject to economic cycles in Mexico and the United States. For example, the cotton boom that resulted from World War I quickly came to an end in 1919 when the price hit bottom and countless migrant workers were left stranded without jobs or transportation. Many of these displaced workers eventually ended up in *barrios* in urban areas. Others shared a similar fate later due to the fall of copper prices, the decline in railroad construction, and, of course, the Great Depression.

It should be kept in mind that many of these *barrios* were originally *sembrados*. Initially, they did not outwardly present the ambience of many urban *barrios* of today; rather, their appearance was basically rural Mexican in nature, i.e., small houses (in some cases, *jacalitos*) lying in open fields, in former *sembrados*, or adjacent to growing fields. More elaborate houses, some of adobe, were gradually built, many in stages as the economics of the people would allow.*

It has been found that, historically, the institutions (including social agencies) with which the people of the *barrios* have had to deal, have generally been insensitive to or ignorant of their sensibilities. The account of one *anciano* relates only one of many examples of this which surfaced in the oral histories of what Galarza (1970) refers to as "institutional deviancy." The confrontation that the *anciano* describes stemmed from an intolerable water situation in Phoenix, Arizona, in 1945, when one faucet attached to a single portable water tank was the only water source for an entire *barrio*. The Mexican Americans of the *barrio*, together with several black residents of the area, organized a "Citizens' Club" and went to the City Water Department to ask that something be done to remedy the situation:

> *Pues como una táctica nos hicieron que fueramos allá a reportar porqué queríamos agua. Pero en lugar de reportar uno lo que quería, porqué quería agua, nos hacían preguntas necias — que si teníamos coches, si teníamos burros, si teníamos vacas, chivas. Les dije, 'Pueden ustedes oirme unas cuantas palabras para que les digan a los oficials' — pues la muchacha que hablaba español ahí— 'No,' me dijo. 'Bueno,' le dije, 'entonces muchas gracias porque siempre le voy a decir: el agua que queremos es para nuestros hijos, no para los burros, ni los coches, ni los animales — es para la salud de las criaturas, y para eso queremos el agua. Es para el bienestar de la familia.' No dijo nada. Luego dije yo, 'Vale más que nos vayamos de aquí, estar aquí como tontos, no nos oyen, no nos quieren atender. Pues que vamos a gritar? No!' Yo no más eso le dije, y nos vinimos todos.*

> Well, as a ruse, they made us go down to report why we wanted water. But instead of letting us tell them why, they would ask us a lot of foolish questions—did we have cars, donkeys, cows, or sheep? I told them, 'Listen to me a second so you can tell these officials—' but the woman who spoke Spanish there said, 'No.'

---

*The historical research was done by Ramon Favela for a study of paint inhalation in the context of the *barrio*. See the reference, Montiel *et al.* (1976), at the end of this paper.

'Very well,' I said, 'then thank you, because I am still going to tell you that the water we want is for our children, not for cars or the animals. It's for the health of our children and the well-being of our families.' She kept silent. Then I said, 'It's no use staying here. They won't even pay any attention to us. And are we going to start yelling? No!' That's all I said, and we left.

During the same time that the Mexican American people of this *barrio* were asking City Hall for some type of moral commitment, a group of Anglos prepared a booklet describing Phoenix, including the *barrio*. In the section on "Appearance of Phoenix," the booklet described many residential areas as "new and clean" and discussed the "smart cosmopolitan air of the business section." It then proceeded to a description of the *barrio:*

> The dark side of the picture is to be found 'south of the tracks' and particularly in a district inhabited large by Spanish-Americans and known as 'Hollywood.' This is a foul slum, the like of which can probably not be found elsewhere in the United States. Hollywood is free from the land overcrowding so characteristic of slums in Eastern cities. The shacks and shanties have plenty of room around them, but there is no running water and no electricity . . . . Room overcrowding is prevalent, often equalling or surpassing the congestion found in Eastern tenements. Open-pit privies are the rule. Sanitation does not exist. It is a miracle that this area of shacks has not produced an epidemic of major proportions.

The *barrio* people themselves had already recognized their condition and in their own *vocabulario* had labeled the *barrio* as *El Guangoche, El Calcetín, La Garra,* and finally, "Hollywood" or "Little Hollywood" (Montiel *et al.,* 1976).

The exploitation and devastation of Mexican American *barrios* take many forms and shapes even to this day. The expansion of industry and the desire of businessmen to revitalize the inner cities have displaced thousands of Chicanos in urban locales across the Southwest. In Phoenix, for example, over the last few decades we have seen entire *barrios* eliminated by freeway construction, the industrialization of the inner city, airport expansion, utility company construction, urban renewal, and land speculation. The fabric of the community is destroyed and the people are not paid sufficient money to replace their homes. Another form of devastation is the conflict of values between the oppressive Anglo society and the Chicano community which has little control over institutions that affect it. The situation was aptly put not long ago by an elderly woman from a *barrio: "La familia mía es la cosa más importante en mi vida, ahora ya no es así . . . aquí la familia vale poco."* ("My family is the most important thing in my life, but now it is not like this . . . here the family matters little.") To her, when members of the *barrio* place little value on the family, this is a result of outside forces. She says that schools teach values that are opposite those of *la familia.* The Army takes our young men away, she says, and sends them back as alcoholics or drug addicts: *"Cuando se van, son Mexicanos; cuando vuelven, son nada."* ("When they leave, they are Mexicans; when they return, they are nothing.") She

28

believes that young people have lost their identity as *Mexicanos* and that is why they are lost, delinquent, or addicted to drugs. There is a loss of respect for the elders which she labels as "terrible" and pinpoints as a cause of the weakening of the whole community. She concludes that the elders are not able to instill the old values because the young have learned other values from the Anglos.

The Church

In or around almost every *barrio* one finds a Catholic church, one of the symbols that unite and define the Mexican American population. The Church has always had a confusing and contradictory history in the lives of the Mexican people. Ruben Salazar, the late Chicano journalist, put it this way:

> Throughout its history, the Catholic Church in Mexico has been the instrument of reaction, according to most Mexican historians. They cite the facts that the Church opposed the War for Independence, sparked the War of the Reform, and sponsored attempts to place and maintain Maximilian on the throne. The clergy also fought the Revolution of 1910, condemned the Constitution of 1917, and started the *Cristero* uprising a decade later in which militant Catholics burned government schools, dynamited a train, and started a full-scale civil war in which thousands were killed.

This paradox has continued in the United States. The Church is seen by many Chicanos, particularly among the more traditional families, as a source of spiritual comfort in an inhospitable land. The disenchantment with the Church that has existed in Mexico, however, also exists here among Chicanos. This situation is best understood in its historical context because, after the annexation of Mexican territory by the United States, "the Spanish-speaking clergy were gradually but ruthlessly displaced and replaced by the Irish" (Cabrera, 1971). The Irish priests did not understand the culture or traditions of the Southwest and in their belief that "their Church was superior, they made vigorous efforts to stamp out the 'decadent' Catholic practices among the Mexicans in the area" (Cabrera, 1971).

According to Grebler, Moore, and Guzman (1970), the Church was the first institution to develop the pattern of relationships between Mexicans and the dominant institutions in the Southwest. If this is the case, there is some evidence that the Church has served as a primary vehicle for segregation and discrimination. The development of Immaculate Heart of Mary Church, a Spanish-speaking parish in Phoenix, provides a good example of how the process operated in one section of the Southwest. *Alive,* a Phoenix diocesan magazine, traces the beginnings of this church to December 12, 1924 when Pope Pius XI signed a decree establishing a parish to serve the Spanish-speaking people of Maricopa County (including Phoenix). According to the author of the article, Rev. Andre Boulanger (1974), the social, religious, and political upheavals in Mexico and along the border in the late 1910s and early 1920s left thousands of Mexicans homeless. "Many came to the Salt River Valley (Phoenix) to settle and find work in the fields. The sudden increase of people in the valley rendered the work of the priests at St. Mary's (Church) almost impossible because of the sheer numbers involved." It is interesting to note that, prior to the signing of the decree in 1924, a majority of the parishioners of St. Mary's (the first church erected in the Phoenix area) were Mexican and had been attending church there since 1881. They were not newcomers. It is not unreasonable to conclude that the new parish was set up because the Anglo Americans did not want to attend the same church as the Mexicans. A recent study by Montiel (1975) reveals that "one priest and several elderly parishioners insist that it was because Mexicans were made to attend Mass downstairs and were forbidden to go upstairs where Americans heard Mass." An elderly lady revealed her feelings about this issue thus: *"No, no más era porque no había lugar, era porque era de Americanos arriba. Yo tenía siete años en 1922 cuando hice la Primera Comunión allí en el subterraneo."* ("It was not because there was no room, but because the upstairs belonged to the Americans. I was seven years old in 1922 when I made my First Communion there in the basement.") Note that this was in 1922, two years before the papal decree, thus indicating that the Mexican parishioners were in the basement of the church prior to the planning of the new "Mexican church."

Although there have been some changes in the hierarchy with the appointment of Mexican American bishops in the Southwest, the elements of exclusion and racism in the ecclesiastical structure continue to date. Nevertheless, the Chicano population clings to its religious faith as tenaciously as ever, with an estimated 70 to 90 percent of Chicanos identifying themselves as Catholic. It also should be emphasized that there is a small, but significant number of Protestant and Mormon Chicanos in the United States. They have similar problems of prejudice and discrimination within their churches.

Selected Population Characteristics

The historical forces that have created the group we call Chicanos are diverse and complex. It is this complexity and heterogeneity that must be considered in reviewing the demographic data on Chicanos. Octavio Romano (1968), the Chicano anthropologist, said it best: "Multiple histories could hardly have done other than breed complex people and equally complex families." He continues this theme of diversity:

> ... Virtually every Mexican American family takes several forms and includes many types of people, from assimilationist to Chicano to cultural nationalist and through all varieties including *un español* thrown in every now and then ... Mexican American families have individuals who no longer speak Spanish, who speak only Spanish, or who speak a combination of both. In short, the same complexity that is found in the general Mexican American population is also found in the family of virtually every Mexican American.

In the November 1969 survey, the U.S. Bureau of the Census (1971) estimated that there were over five million persons identifying themselves as Mexican Americans or Chicanos; by March 1975 the Bureau (1976) estimated this population had increased to 6.7 million persons. These figures differ from those estimated by such Hispanic organizations as the National Council of La Raza, the Mexican American Legal Defense and Education Fund, the American G.I. Forum, and IMAGE which claim that the Mexican origin population is well over eight million. The discrepancy in estimates led the U.S. Commission on Civil Rights (1974) to report a "significant undercount" greater than the 7.7 percent undercount reported for blacks. From these conservative figures one can estimate that the Chicano population is actually closer to nine million persons or more.

Type of Household

TABLE IV
PERSONS IN HOUSEHOLD WITH HEAD OF MEXICAN ORIGIN BY TYPE OF HOUSEHOLD, FOR THE UNITED STATES MARCH 1974

Type of Household	Mexican Origin
All households (thousands)	1,516
Percent	100.0
Primary Families	89.3
Husband-Wife	73.5
Other Male Head	2.9
Female Head	12.9
Primary Individuals	10.7
Male	6.3
Female	4.4

SOURCE: U.S. Bureau of the Census, *Current Population Reports*, P-20, No. 280, "Persons of Spanish Origin in the United States: March 1974," Table 9, p. 29. Washington, D.C.: Government Printing Office, 1975.

As indicated in Table IV, over 73 percent of households reported in the March 1974 survey were headed by husband and wife, while close to 13 percent were headed by females. These figures have climbed steadily over the last several years.

As of March 1975, it was estimated that there were 4.2 million Chicanos 14 years old and over with considerably more single males (36.2 percent) than females (27.9 percent). Approximately 60 percent of both males and females were married. Indicative of the longer life span of women, 6.3 percent of the women were widowed as opposed to 1.3 percent of the men. It is interesting to note that twice as many women (4.6 percent) as men (2.4 percent) were divorced in 1975, this in contrast to 1972 figures of 23.2 percent for females and 1.5 percent for males (Barcelo, 1977). Not surprisingly, 54 percent of female-headed households were below the poverty line. One positive note is that since 1970 the rate of female-headed Mexican origin households has remained constant.

The 1969 data on language and literacy provide some interesting insights in relation to educational and employment opportunities. In 1969, 72 percent of Mexican Americans reported Spanish as their mother tongue, that is, the language spoken as a child. As a current language, however, only 47 percent reported speaking Spanish at home. The ability to read and write English is of primary importance in this monolingual nation. Slightly more than 95 percent of Mexican Americans between the ages of 10 and 24 years reported that they were literate in English, while 71.5 percent of those age 25 and older so reported. Similarly, Mexican

31

Americans in the 25-34 age group had 10.8 years of education completed, compared to 12.4 years completed by the general population. Mexican Americans over age 35 had a mean education level of 7.3 years completed.

Poverty

Not unexpectedly, the income level for Chicanos falls considerably below that for the general population. The median income for families of Mexican origin in 1974 was $9,498 compared to nearly $13,400 for Anglo families.

TABLE V

INCOME OF FAMILIES WITH HEAD OF MEXICAN ORIGIN, ALSO OF FAMILIES OF WHITE RACE MARCH 1974

Family Head and Race	Median Family Income	Percent with Family Income Below $4,000	Percent with Income of $15,000 or more
Mexican	$ 9,498	15	20
White	$13,356	7	42

SOURCE: U.S. Bureau of the Census, *Current Population Reports*, No. 283, Advance Report, August 1975, p. 20.

As Table V shows, in 1974 more than twice as many Mexican American families, as Anglo families, were below the level of $4,000 per year; conversely, more than twice as many Anglo families, as Mexican American families, were above the $15,000 annual income level. When one considers that Mexican American families are larger, on the average, than Anglo families, the differences become even more significant. Despite the rhetoric of the civil rights movement, the differential between families of Mexican origin and Anglo families has remained steady at .72 over the past five years.

Vast pockets of poverty, especially among Mexican American migrant and seasonal farmworkers, still exist. The conventional interpretation among many social scientists is that poverty and related problems among Chicanos result from "cultural disadvantage." According to this interpretation, it is only through social and educational programs designed to accommodate individuals to "acceptable" standards of behavior that Chicanos can escape the "culture of poverty." In other words, individuals—not institutions—need corrective intervention. It is estimated that approximately 23 percent of the Mexican American population, compared to 8.9 percent of Anglos, have incomes below the poverty line (Barcelo, 1977). Poverty breeds not only illness and poor health, poor education, malnutrition, and social disdain, but also has other consequences that ultimately affect the entire society—segregation and racial/ethnic prejudice. One example is found in the following viewpoint of the head of the National Association of Home Builders (reported in the *San Jose Mercury*, San Jose, California, January 8, 1970):

> Affluent Santa Clara County (California) is mired in a severe housing crisis that hurts the poor . . . and creates segregation and ghettos. It is driving the affluent and poor, and the Anglo-Saxon

majority and the Mexican American minority, farther and farther apart . . . . There has been an increasing inability of the housing market to respond to the needs of low-income households.

In an analysis of participation rates of persons of Hispanic heritage in welfare programs, Barcelo (1977) found that, in 1973, 14.4 percent of Chicano families were recipients of Aid to Families with Dependent Children (AFDC), a slight decrease in the percentage participating since 1967. Unfortunately, many public assistance programs do not keep statistics by ethnic groups, and thus a complete account of the degree of help provided to Mexican Americans is not available. One could speculate, however, that Chicanos do not receive a proportionate share of assistance compared to other disadvantaged groups.

In sharp contrast to the "culture of poverty" proponents, Briggs (1973), a Texas economist, argues that the economic plight of rural Chicanos presents "a classic example of administered social oppression." Public policy that has denied Chicanos their equal rights, he asserts, is the direct and principal cause of rural poverty among Chicanos.

Briggs identifies two basic sources of public policy that maintain the advantage of large agribusiness over economically disadvantaged Chicanos. First, their economic plight is closely linked to the overall economic dependence of Mexico on the United States. Mexico's inability to support its populace has forced a continual flow of migration of Mexicans to this country. The United States, in turn, has exploited this situation. The best example is the *bracero* program, a cooperative venture between Mexico and the United States which enabled millions of Mexican workers to enter this country on a temporary basis and insured that agribusiness would have a virtually inexhaustible supply of cheap labor. Furthermore, public laws encourage the hiring of undocumented workers by putting the onus of responsibility on them rather than on employers who not only exploit their labor but also keep wages at a less than equitable level.

The second source identified by Briggs is the peculiar practice of making farmworkers the exception to almost all statutory enactments. Minimum wage coverage, unemployment insurance coverage, workmen's compensation, and the right of collective bargaining are some of the more salient examples in this regard. Opponents of the inclusion of farmworkers have argued that it would cause inflation and hasten automation, inevitably reducing the jobs available.

In summary, when one considers the rapid rate of growth of this population, the increasing rate of immigration, the youthful age of the population, its low level of education and income, and its alienation from the dominant society, the crisis facing both this population and the United States is evident. What is also becoming more clear is the potential of this population for political influence and power.

Mental Health

The demographic characteristics that are attached to their poverty status, such as low income and education levels, poor housing, and a virtual absence of political power, are only part of the objective situation of many Chicanos. Padilla and Ruiz (1973) identify various other high stress indicators that are shared by many Chicanos, particularly the poor:

- Poor communication skills in English.
- Survival of traits from a rural agrarian culture that are relatively ineffective in an urban technological society.
- The necessity (for some) of seasonal migration.
- The very stressful problem of acculturation to a society that often appears prejudicial, hostile, and rejecting.

At first glance, it would appear that Chicanos would be eager to receive the multitude of services advertised by the mental health establishment. After all, many of the high stress indicators are associated with the problems of adjustment in society. *This, however, is not the case.*

Why do Spanish-speaking people receive the least amount of mental health services even though they are subjected to numerous high stress indicators? Two principal explanations are offered for this peculiar situation. One is that Spanish-speaking people use alternative avenues for mental health services that are indigenous to their culture. These alternatives include folk medicine and faith healing. While the empirical evidence to reject or substantiate this explanation is lacking, expert opinion rejects it (Padilla and Ruiz, 1973). A second explanation for the underutilization of mental health services seems more reasonable in light of the stance of the social science literature vis-a-vis Chicanos. According to this explanation, staff and institutions "discourage the delivery of services to the Spanish-speaking" (Torrey, 1970). This is done in a variety of ways, many of them so embedded in the inequity of the system that therapists rarely recognize the nature of the oppression. For example, when a Spanish-speaking patient finally comes to a clinic and finds that no one there speaks Spanish, rarely do therapists and administrators view this as an act of institutional exclusion. Similar but more severe problems arise because of inaccurate diagnostic and treatment decisions based on either cultural or class differences (Torrey, 1970). Torrey identifies three variables that add to the difficulties Spanish-speaking people face when attempting to receive services: prejudice, social distance, and reliance on a traditional physical symptom model of inquiry that omits consideration of potentially significant ethnographic data.

The unequal access to mental health services is only part of the problem, If, all of a sudden, Chicanos flooded existing mental health facilities, the inadequate and faulty knowledge about them would result in services that would be inconsistent with their needs and wishes. *It is the control of the diagnostic and treatment paradigms more than the underutilization of mental health services that alarms many Chicanos.* Directly and indirectly, the challenge to the social sciences and the Chicano lies here.

Toward a Chicano Perspective

Not surprisingly, because of the diversity of the Chicano population both spatially and temporally, a variety of perspectives are evident in the Chicano community, ranging from assimilation-acculturation to bicultural accommodation to historical sequential. This brief discussion presents only the major perspectives that have emerged.

Perhaps the most evident, although currently not the most popular, is the assimilation-acculturation perspective. The basic argument centers around the process of assimilation, and its most articulate spokesman has been the sociologist Julian Samora. The individual is said to progress

through a four-stage process (Samora and Lamanna, 1967):
1) Accommodation where there is a minimal acceptance of the immigrant group that is limited to physical integrity and well-being.
2) Economic integration where the concern is with the immigrant group's adaptation to the host society.
3) Cultural integration where there is a convergence of the material, behavioral, and symbolic elements of the two cultures.
4) Social integration where there is increasing involvement of the two groups in a common network of social relationships involving mutual acceptance.

The central thesis of this view seems to be that Chicanos must acculturate from the traditional culture to the modern American culture if they hope to make it in this society. Heller (1966), the Anglo sociologist, in discussing the structural organization of the Mexican American family and its adherence to traditional forms, states that the latter "provide stumbling blocks to the values conducive to mobility," i.e., achievement, independence, and deferred gratification. The assumptions and inherent intervention policies of the assimilation-acculturation model can be better understood from Clark (1959):

There are features of American life that *barrio* people like and want for themselves, features which serve to motivate people toward change to Anglo patterns . . . They want the higher social status which comes to those who learn and practice Anglo ways . . .

Thus, on close examination, the assimilation-acculturation perspective becomes the medical model perspective in disguise—it is a non-Chicano perspective. It is only by becoming "American" that Chicanos can escape poverty. For Chicanos, the integration perspective has been a dead-end strategy for political and economic integration into the American system, as it has been for the developing countries of Latin America.

Partly as a reaction to the academic stranglehold of the assimilation-acculturation model and partly as a result of the political alienation of Chicanos in this country, other perspectives have emerged. Although they differ in ideology and content, they all challenge the academic interpretations of the past and rely heavily on historical interpretations (for only through history can one speak of perspective).

George I. Sanchez, educator and early advocate for the Chicano movement, shifted the blame for academic difficulties from Chicano youngsters to the school system. He argued that schools needed to recognize the socio-cultural differences between the pupil and the school in designing the curriculum. In *Forgotten Americans* (1940), Sanchez explained that the problem of the Spanish-speaking in the United States was not strictly "bilingual," but was one of cultural contact and persistent conflict with the dominant society. The relations between the United States and Mexico, historically, have been grounded in conflict and only through an analysis of the various phases of this conflict—spatial and temporal—could one hope to understand the cultural differences that have persisted between Chicanos and Anglos. The perspective of Sanchez is best exemplified in his views on education where he advocated programs based on the child's cultural differences and geared to his or her customs and traditions, to his or her language and historical background. He argued that the United States assumed a social responsibility because of the conquest and annexation. Sanchez stands out in broad profile, for his work pioneered many ideas in education that have yet to be fully appreciated or accepted by the dominant society.

Quinto Sol Publications, under the leadership of Octavio Romano, initiated the arduous task of articulating what has proved to be one of the most significant academic Chicano movements to date. Romano's purge of the sociology and anthropology of the Mexican American, like that of Sanchez in psychology and education, set the stage for a new perspective to emerge. This time, however, unlike the time in which Sanchez produced his farsighted work, others have followed suit. Romano's critique of the literature focused on the idea of the Traditional Culture which, according to him, depicts Mexican Americans as "passive containers and retainers of culture." Traditional Culture, Romano said, has been used to describe the foundations of Mexican American culture and historically document Chicano existence. The result has been that Chicanos have not been seen as participants of history until they have undergone acculturation. In his systematic critique of the social sciences, Romano concluded that the idea of the historical culture must be substituted for the notion of Traditional Culture and its bias toward assimilation. Romano's historical culture stresses the pluralistic nature of the Chicano. In developing this notion, Romano, like Sanchez, relies on historical evidence to support his argument.

To the heterogeneous philosophical antecedents of the Chicano such as Indianism, historical confrontation, and Mexican-based cultural nationalism, Romano added the grower-*campesino* struggle, the nationalism of Reyes Lopez Tijerina, the nationalistic movement of Rodolfo "Corky" Gonzales, the student movement, and the Chicano studies movement. In his analysis, Romano showed how Chicanos have been participants in the historical process, creators of social systems, and creators of diverse forms of art; how they have actively engaged in political and social confrontation; and how they have developed their own system of nationality. Perhaps the most important point he makes is that people are evaluated according to the definitions thrust upon them (Romano, 1968, 1969, 1971). That the definitions thus imposed have been less than complimentary is obvious from the literature.

La Academia de la Nueva Raza, under the direction of Tomas Atencio, has been collecting oral histories, folklore, poetry, and music from the rural areas of New Mexico which beautifully describe the life of the people there (Arellano, 1972). Atencio's work is an attempt to find ways of developing a body of knowledge that reflects the Chicano experience, life styles, and identity. Atencio (1972) believes that Chicanos "must turn this body of knowledge into an educational process of *concientizacion* to develop a humanity—or better, to rehumanize humanity."

Closely allied ideologically with Atencio's work, Ernesto Galarza, the dean of Chicano scholars, urges that Chicanos engage in "functional" research—a type of research that studies "the realities of the Chicano existence." Galarza (1970) suggests that Chicanos should study "institutional deviancy" in an effort to change the manner in which institutions in this country have served them. He defines "institutional deviancy" as "the tendency of an institution to depart from its moral commitment and from all those things it was set up to do."

There are, of course, numerous other Chicano scholars who have initiated other perspectives, most notable of whom are the neo-colonialists who argue that Chicanos, like all Third World people, are a colonized minority in their own conquered land. Historian Rodolfo Acuna (1972) has been a leading spokesman of this perspective.

Conclusion

The study of Chicanos in the United States has been dominated by a theoretical model which defines them essentially as "sick." This externally controlled model has distorted their history and has forced them to live someone else's experience. Chicanos must respond to this state of crisis in an original and creative manner. The rewriting of their history and the reinterpretation of their position in American society will demand new and innovative uses of social science research that liberates and unifies rather than domesticates and divides Chicano communities.

That part of the United States where most Mexican immigrants have settled once belonged to Mexico. The historical effects of the conquest, coupled with the region's proximity to Mexico, serve as constant reinforcers of the Mexican influence. In some areas of the Southwest more than others, Mexican culture has lingered on despite the overwhelming dominance of Anglo society. The relatively small number of Mexicans in this region at the time of the conquest has been steadily augmented by Mexican immigrants, especially since the Revolution of 1910. The demand for labor, created by World War I and the subsequent prosperity of the 1920s, maintained a massive flow of Mexicans into the United States until the crash of 1929. Massive deportations, legal and illegal, plus the hard times created by the Depression, restricted the flow until the labor demands of World War II and the development of agribusiness attracted an unprecedented number of Mexican workers. The influx was drastically curtailed in 1954 by "Operation Wetback." A smaller but steady immigration has continued to date.

It is obvious that the history and current existence of Chicanos is inextricably tied to Mexico. It is interesting that, with rare exception, the Mexican Government has failed to recognize and act upon its link with Chicanos in this country. The U.S. Government recognizes this and much of its abuse of Chicanos (and undocumented aliens from Mexico) can be partly explained by Mexico's refusal to accept its responsibility for the millions of Chicanos who share a like history and identity. Other countries, such as Japan and Israel, maintain a link with their people because they have found it advantageous.

Expecting governments to reverse public policies because they are unjust, however, is at best a shaky premise. The history of the United States reveals that changes have come only through the dedicated efforts of individuals and groups willing to confront established interests. Because of this, it will be primarily through the efforts of Chicanos themselves that any substantive changes will occur.

REFERENCES

Acuna, Rodolfo. *Occupied America: The Chicano Struggle Toward Freedom.* San Francisco: Canfield Press, 1972.

Arellano, Estevan (ed.). *Entre Verde y Seco.* Dixon, New Mexico: La Academia de la Nueva Raza,* 1972.

Atencio, Tomas. Mental health and the Spanish-speaking. *In* Susan Riley (ed.), *Mental Health Planning Conference for the Spanish-Speaking: Proceedings, January 11-12, 1972.* Rockville, Maryland: National Institute of Mental Health, 1972.

Baratz, Steven S., and Baratz, Joan C. Early childhood intervention: the social science base of institutional racism. *Harvard Educational Review,* Winter 1970.

Barcelo, Cosme. An analysis of participation rates of persons of Hispanic heritage in welfare programs. In *Proceedings of the Symposium on Chicanos and Welfare.* Washington, D.C.: National Council of La Raza, 1977.

Boulanger, Rev. Andre, V.F. Mother church to the Mexicans. *Alive* (family magazine of the Diocese of Phoenix, Arizona), November 1974.

Briggs, Vernon M., Jr. *Chicanos and Rural Poverty.* Baltimore: Johns Hopkins University Press, 1973.

Cabrera, Y. Arturo. *Emerging Faces: the Mexican Americans.* San Jose State College, San Jose, California: William C. Brown Company Publishers, 1971.

Clark, Margaret. *Health in the Mexican American Culture: A Community Study.* Berkeley: University of California Press, 1959.

Daniels, Roger. Racism and immigration restriction. *In* Harold D. Woodman (ed.), *Forums in History.* St. Charles, Missouri: Forum Press, 1974.

Galarza, Ernesto. Institutional deviancy: the Mexican American experience. *In* Stanley Boucher (ed.), *Mexican American Mental Health Issues: Present Realities and Future Strategies.* Papers from a conference sponsored by the Western Interstate Commission for Higher Education (WICHE), June 10-12, 1970.

Grebler, Leo; Moore, Joan W.; and Guzman, Ralph C. *The Mexican American People: The Nation's Second Largest Minority.* New York: the Free Press, 1970.

Hayden, Robert G. Spanish Americans of the Southwest: life style patterns and their implications. *Welfare in Review,* April 1966.

Heller, Celia S. *Mexican American Youth: Forgotten Youth at the Crossroads.* New York: Random House, 1966.

Madsen, William. *The Mexican Americans of South Texas.* New York: Holt, Rinehart, and Winston, Inc., 1964.

Manuel, Herschel T. *The Spanish-Speaking Children of the Southwest— Their Education and the Public Welfare.* Austin: University of Texas Press, 1965.

Matza, David. *Becoming Deviant.* Englewood Cliffs, New Jersey: Prentice-Hall, Inc., 1969.

Miller, Henry. Social work in the black ghetto: the new colonialism. *Social Work,* July 1969, *14,* 3.

Montiel, Miguel *et al.* Paint inhalation among Chicano *barrio* youth: an exploratory study. Prepared by Valle del Sol, Inc., for the National Institute on Drug Abuse, June 1976.

Montiel, Yvonne de la Torre. The genesis of Immaculate Heart Church: mother church to the Mexicans. Unpublished paper, 1975.

Ortega y Gasset, Jose. *Man and People.* New York: W.W. Norton and Company, 1957.

Padilla, A.M., and Ruiz, R.A. *Latino Mental Health: A Review of the Literature.* DHEW Publication No. (HSM) 73-9143. Washington, D.C.: Government Printing Office, 1973.

Ramirez, Raul *et al.* Undocumented aliens in the Southwest. Unpublished paper, 1977.

Romano, Octavio I. The anthropology and sociology of the Mexican Americans: the distortion of Mexican American history. *El Grito* (Quinto Sol Publications), Fall 1968.

_____ . The historical and intellectual presence of Mexican Americans. *El Grito* (Quinto Sol Publications), Winter 1969.

Romano, Octavio I. (ed.). *El Espejo: Selected Mexican American Literature.* Berkeley, California: Quinto Sol Publications, 1969.

_____ . *Voices: Readings from El Grito: A Journal of Contemporary Mexican American Thought, 1967-1971.* Berkeley, California: Qunito Sol Publications, 1971.

Samora, Julian. *Los Mojados: The Wetback Story.* Notre Dame, Indiana: University of Notre Dame Press, 1971.

Samora, Julian and Lamanna, Richard A. Mexican Americans in a Midwest metropolis: a study of East Chicago. *Mexican American Study Project, Advance Report No. 8.* University of California at Los Angeles, Graduate School of Business Administration, Division of Research, 1967.

Sanchez, George I. *Forgotten People: A Study of New Mexicans.* Albuquerque: University of New Mexico Press, 1940.

Saunders, Lyle. The social history of Spanish-speaking people in the Southwestern United States since 1846. Paper presented at the 4th Regional Conference, Southwest Council on Education of Spanish-Speaking People, January 23-25, 1950.

Torrey, E. Fuller. The irrelevancy of traditional mental health services for urban Mexican Americans. Paper presented at the meeting of the American Orthopsychiatry Association, San Francisco, California, March 1970.

U.S. Bureau of the Census. *Current Population Reports,* Series P-20, No. 213, "Persons of Spanish Origin in the United States, November 1969." Washington, D.C.: Government Printing Office, 1971.

_____ . *Current Population Reports,* P-20, No. 290, "Persons of Spanish Origin in the United States: March 1975." Washington, D.C.: Government Printing Office, 1976.

U.S. Commission on Civil Rights. *Counting the Forgotten: the 1970 Census Count of Persons of Spanish-Speaking Background in the United States.* Washington, D.C.: Government Printing Office, April 1974.

Valentine, Charles A. *Culture and Poverty.* Chicago: University of Chicago Press, 1968.

INTERGENERATIONAL SOURCES OF ROLE CONFLICT IN CUBAN MOTHERS

Jose Szapocznik and Carroll Truss

The present study arose from the authors' concern over the epidemic abuse of sedatives and tranquilizers and frequent overdoses of these drugs by Cuban middle-aged women (Ladner, Page, and Lee, 1975). Clinical observations revealed that the use and abuse of such drugs were most prevalent among middle-aged white Cuban women with adolescent children. It was also observed that these women were manifesting conflicts resulting from the usual family intergenerational differences (Spiegel, 1970) and, more importantly, conflicts introduced by differential degrees of acculturation within the nuclear family (Szapocznik, Scopetta, Kurtines, and Aranalde, 1978). The data presented here are not related to drug use and misuse by these mothers, but to the sources and nature of the conflicts they experienced. The data on drug abuse are presented elsewhere (Szapocznik, Scopetta, and Tillman, 1978). It is noteworthy, however, that about 67 percent of the mothers in the study reported some current use of sedatives and tranquilizers.

The Stresses of Acculturation

Many studies have documented the high rates of behavioral disorders among immigrants, and there has been increased interest in identifying the factors related to these disorders (Mezey, 1960; Al-Issa, 1970; Berry and Annis, 1974). According to Kelly (1973), the acculturation process results in the disruption of the family which in turn leads to behavioral disorders in family members. Clinical observations within the Cuban immigrant community indicate that family disruption occurs as a result of intergenerational differences in acculturation (Szapocznik, Scopetta, and King, 1978). When youngsters acculturate more rapidly than their parents, intergenerational acculturation differences develop. According to these authors, this results in an exacerbated intergenerational acculturation gap that constitutes the essence of family disruption in first-generation Cuban immigrant families.

Generally in Latin cultures, the weight of the preservation of the family falls on the mother (Padilla and Ruiz, 1973). Therefore, as Cuban families become disrupted, Cuban mothers are likely to experience stress. It has been amply documented that family structure and family roles change for Spanish American immigrant groups as a result of their migration to the United States (e.g., Penalosa, 1968; Goldsen, Mills, and Senior, 1972; and Szapocznik, 1976). These changes in family role definitions may be resulting in role conflicts, particularly for mothers since they are primarily responsible for preservation of the family.

This work was supported in part by Grant No. 5H81 DA 91696 from the National Institute on Drug Abuse, Rockville, Maryland.

Gerth and Mills (1953) point out that cultures in which there is a loose unity of social structure, such as exists in the United States, are likely to result in a wider variation of expectations and increased personality conflicts. When social institutions exist autonomously in a society, roles are more likely to be conflicting. It would appear then that role theory may provide a heuristic model for an understanding of the stresses experienced by Cuban mothers in Miami, Florida, and shed light on the etiology of drug abuse among these women.

Szapocznik *et al.* (1978b) found that intergenerational differences in behavioral acculturation arise as the acculturation process proceeds. These differences may be at the crux of clinically observed family conflict in acculturating families. Many family traditions come under close scrutiny and require redefinition as families acculturate. One traditional bastion of Cuban family life—the mother's role in the family—seems to be most challenged as a result of this process of acculturation. During this process the mother experiences role conflict as well as role stress. In order to document the intergenerational conflicts in role definition as perceived by Cuban mothers, a study was conducted on the expectations that they perceived relevant others held for them, the perceived legitimacy of these expectations, and the sanctions attached to non-compliance with them.

This paper attempts to identify one process that may explain how the familial pathology of intergenerational differences in acculturation affects Cuban mothers and becomes a source of role conflict and role stress which eventuates in their symptomatic behavior, their use and abuse of sedatives and tranquilizers.

Data reported in this paper were collected as part of a programmatic series of studies aimed at: (1) investigating the patterns of expectations that Cuban mothers perceived as held for them by close family members around relevant child rearing issues; (2) cross-validating the theory of role conflict resolution developed by Gross, McEacher, and Mason (1958, 1966) with a population of Cuban mothers with adolescent children; (3) developing an index to identify mothers who face the risk of severe role stress and family disruption; (4) investigating the relationship of time spent in the United States and acculturation to the mode of role stress and role conflict resolution; and (5) relating role stress, mothers' characteristics, level of acculturation, and mode of role conflict resolution to the use of sedatives and tranquilizers.

This paper presents the patterns of expectations, legitimacy, and sanctions perceived by Cuban mothers as held for them by close family members. After a perusal of the literature on role conflicts and role stress and on the basis of the theory of role conflict resolution developed by Gross *et al.*, these three variables—expectations, legitimacy, and sanctions—were chosen for careful scrutiny because they appeared to be most relevant in understanding the nature of role stress in the subject population.

Method

Subjects

Subjects in this study were 110 white Cuban-born women who had lived in Cuba through age 16, had left Cuba after 1959, lived in Miami at the time of data collection (1975-1976), and had at least one child between the ages of 12 and 24.

Referrals for the study were obtained in several ways. Forty-one subjects were referred by various social service agencies. With these, there was an implication that psycho-social problems either existed or had been prevalent shortly before referral. Twenty-nine mothers were referred by mental health professionals from among their friends or acquaintances. For these, there was no reason to believe that serious problems existed. Thirty-three mothers were referred by previous participants in the study. Referral data were missing on seven mothers.

In order to obtain subject referrals, various community agencies were contacted. Agency representatives were informed that the investigators were conducting a study about family problems confronting Cuban mothers with adolescent children. Criteria for participation in the study were also explained. When prospective subjects were referred, they were screened to assess whether or not they met the criteria. Only those mothers who met the criteria were asked to volunteer for the study, and an appointment was made for a home visit during which the research interview was conducted. In many instances, more than one home visit was necessary to complete data collection. Interviewing time ranged from two to seven hours, although most interviews were completed in about three hours.

In order to define the population under study more specifically, information was collected on age, marital status, religious affiliation, socio-economic status of the head of the household at the time of this research study and at the time of departure from Cuba, length of stay in Dade County (Florida) and in the United States, language preference and proficiency, number of children, and drug usage. These data were missing for seven mothers.

Ages of the mothers ranged from 30 to 58 years, with a mean of 43 and a standard deviation of 6.4. Most were married at the time of the interviews (N=85), while seven were divorced, seven widowed, three separated, and one was married but her husband was still in Cuba. The overwhelming majority were of the Catholic faith (N=97), while six were Protestant.

In order to obtain a measure of socio-economic status, the two factor index of Hollingshead (1957) was used. This index combines educational and occupational levels of the head of the household, providing a five-level measure of socio-economic status. Level 1 represents the highest status; Level 5, the lowest. The following levels were reported by the subjects: Level 1, 19.6 percent; Level 2, 3.9 percent; Level 3, 25.5 percent; Level 4, 22.5 percent; and Level 5, 28.5 percent.

The length of time the subjects had lived in this country ranged from eight to 240 months, with a mean of 122 months, a standard deviation of 55, and a mode of 156. The subject population in this study can be described as "relatively Cuban" with regard to their language preference and proficiency. When asked "Which language do you prefer to speak?", 75.5 percent responded "Spanish all the time," while 18.2 percent responded "Spanish most of the time," 6.4 percent said "Spanish and English equally," and no one preferred to speak English over Spanish. With regard to proficiency in English, 4.5 percent reported speaking it very well; 11.8 percent, well; 28.2 percent, average; 20.9 percent, poor; and 34.5 percent, very poor. With regard to proficiency in Spanish, 43.5 percent reported speaking it very well; 55.5 percent, well; and one percent, average. Further illustrating the subjects' use of Spanish, 83.6 percent reported speaking it at home all the time, 12.7 percent spoke it most of the time, and only 3.6 percent said they spoke Spanish and English equally at home. Finally, 79.1 percent reported speaking Spanish all the time with their friends, 15.5 percent spoke it most of the time with their friends, and 5.5 percent reported speaking just as much Spanish as English with their friends.

The subjects' children ranged widely in age—from one to 36 years—although most were in the 12-24 age range. All of the subjects had at least one child in the 12-24 age range since this was one criterion for inclusion in the study. Only 15 percent of the subjects had one child, while 35 percent had two children, 25.5 percent had three, 12.5 percent had four, and 11 percent had more than four.

With regard to the use of psychoactive medication, 33.5 percent of the mothers interviewed reported no current use. *However, the remaining 66.5 percent reported some current use of sedatives and tranquilizers.* The drugs of choice for these mothers were Valium and Librium which 76 percent cited as a primary drug of use, either with or without a prescription.

Interviewers

Data were collected by three interviewers. They were Cuban-born women who were between the ages of 22 and 25, were fluent in Spanish and English, and had received considerable training in interviewing skills. One had a master's degree in social work, while the others were working toward master's degrees in social work or psychology. In order to insure reliabilities among interviewers, they were trained extensively on all instruments requiring judgments until their judgments correlated at least .80 with one another and with those of the study directors.

Role Conflicts

Perception of expectations. The concept of role conflict has been variously defined by different writers. In this study the focus was on perceived contradictory expectations or demands. This resulted from requirements of the larger study, of which data in this paper are only one part. For the larger study on role conflict resolution, it was assumed that a theoretical model predicting a person's behavior when that person is exposed to contradictory demands must be based on the assumption that the person perceives the role conflict (Gross *et al.,* 1958). Relevant others may actually hold contradictory demands for a person, but if the person is unaware of these demands, he or she cannot consider alternative solutions. For this reason, the focus of investigation in this paper is also on perceived contradictory demands. Thus, a role conflict is defined when a person perceives *incompatible* (contradictory) *expectations* (demands).

Intra-role conflicts. Role conflict may arise when a person is exposed to incompatible expectations as a consequence of his or her occupancy of a single role position (e.g., Parsons, 1951; Gross *et al.,* 1958, 1966). Sarbin and Allen (1968, p. 540) write that intra-role conflict "involves contradictory expectations held by two or more groups of relevant others responding to the same role." The present study investigates the intra-role conflicts experienced by Cuban mothers with respect to their role as mothers.

Content. What constitutes a role conflict? According to the definition developed by Gross *et al.* (1958), role conflict is any situation in which a person perceives that he or she is confronted with incompatible demands or expectations. Since this study was primarily concerned with identifying patterns of expectations around role conflict situations, it was desirable to design a procedure for identifying areas of possible intergenerational role conflicts which were both relevant to the population of Cuban mothers and occurred frequently in this population. Family-related issues and family members seemed particularly relevant in eliciting intergenerational sources of conflict because "performance in those organizations which require high allegiance and devotion such as the family . . . is more likely to affect self-conception and the total self-image than performance in those organizations which are normally less important" (Hass, 1964, p. 9). In particular, with a Cuban subject population, values and ties are deep and pervasive—the traditional Cuban family structure, more than that of Anglo families, requires high allegiance and devotion from its members (Scopetta and Alegre, 1976).

A three-step pilot study was conducted to identify possible areas of role conflict. In the first step, eight white Cuban-born women were interviewed in their homes. These women had been in Cuba through age 16, now lived in Miami, had children ages 13 to 24, had at one time requested outpatient services from the Spanish Family Guidance Clinic,* and were between the ages of 30 and 55. The purpose of the interviews was to assess the kinds of family conflicts perceived by these mothers as affecting their families and other families they knew about. Five major areas of conflict emerged which were, in order of importance:

1. Kinds of friends the children have.
2. The children's lack of respect for authority.
3. Dangers to which the children are exposed, such as drugs, violence, and rape.
4. The father's lack of involvement in the children's upbringing.
5. The welfare and care of grandparents.

In the second step, six additional interviews were conducted in order to assess the generalizability of these findings to the target population. These six subjects met the criteria previously described, except that they had never been in treatment before. Subjects were approached by a Cuban white middle-aged interviewer in the lobbies of four Cuban medical clinics. The interviews were structured so that each of the previous five issues was discussed with each subject. Issues 1, 2, and 3 were reported as areas of conflict by five of the six interviewees; Issue 4 by four of the six; and Issue 5 by three of the six. On the basis of these limited results and in an effort to limit the scope of the study, the first four issues of conflict reported by the majority of the six interviewees were chosen for investigation.

The third step of the study further assessed the extent to which the four content areas thus selected appeared to be important to the target population. This substudy was carried out concurrently with a scale construction substudy in which 177 Cuban-born women were asked to indicate the extent to which they felt obligated to do or not do 45 different role-relevant behaviors. Among these items were:

A. Looking after the type of friends their children have.
B. Imparting respect for authority to their children.

---

*An outpatient mental health, drug and alcohol abuse treatment center located in the Little Havana area at 2121 S.W. 27th Avenue, Miami.

C. Protecting their children from dangers of the streets (e.g., violence, drugs, rape, etc.).
D. Getting their husbands more involved in the upbringing of the children.

The percentage of women responding that they "absolutely should" or "absolutely should not" do A, B, C, and D were 74 percent, 82, 89, and 79, respectively. In all four instances, most mothers responded "absolutely should," implying that strong feelings about these four items were prevalent in the target population.

The investigation of the mothers' mode of role conflict resolution in four different family content areas was expected to allow cross-validation of the findings across a range of family issues. It should be noted that two of these—B and D—involve possible conflicts with the locus primarily within the family nucleus. The others—A and C—involve possible conflicts with the locus ranging from inside to outside the family nucleus. Therefore, B and D are referred to as intra-family issues, whereas A and C are referred to as extra-family or ecological issues.

Relevant others. The identification of role conflict situations presupposes the identification of incompatible expectations perceived by the mother as held for her by relevant others. As indicated earlier, family issues and family members probably are responsible for most conflicts central to the individual's functioning. This is expected to be especially true among Cuban families in which relationships are deep and pervasive. Having identified four major areas of concern which were also areas of frequently occurring family conflicts in the target population, it became necessary to identify the appropriate "relevant others" whom the subjects might perceive as holding incompatible expectations for them in these areas. In general, the most relevant roles complementary to the role of a Cuban mother are those of her children, her husband, and her parents. Therefore, these three sets of complementary family roles were investigated. One additional "general" category was included for which there existed no theoretical rationale but which seemed to warrant empirical assessment. This category was called "most other people you know."

Assessing role conflicts. As has been indicated, a role conflict is said to exist when incompatible demands or expectations are perceived by the subject. In order to identify these in each of the four family issues under investigation, each subject was asked to indicate her perception of what was expected of her as follows:

DO YOU THINK: Your children
       Your husband
       Your parents
       Most other people you know

EXPECT YOU TO: Look after the kinds of friends your children have?
        Impart respect for authority to your children?
        Protect your children from dangers of the streets, such as drugs, violence, and rape?
        Involve your husband in the rearing of your children?

Whenever demands within an issue were perceived to be in opposition to (incompatible with) each other, a role conflict situation was defined as occurring for that issue. If a mother perceived that a relevant other

46

(husband, child, parents, others she knew) expected her to look after the kinds of friends her children have (Issue A, cultural direction), this was noted as E; whereas if she perceived that a relevant other expected her *not* to (Issue A, counter-cultural direction), this was noted as E', and similarly for the remaining issues. If a mother perceived that one relevant other held expectations E(A) for her while another relevant other held expectation E'(A) for her, then the perception of these incompatible demands was said to constitute a role conflict, and similarily for the remaining issues. By this procedure it was possible to analyze the data on perceived demands of relevant others with respect to any given issue and reduce the situation to a dichotomy: either there was a role conflict with respect to the issue or there was not. *Unprimed notation* on perceived expectations indicates that they are in accord with Cuban cultural norms. *Primed notation* indicates they are contrary to these norms.

Legitimacy of Expectations

The emphasis here is on the perceived legitimacy of expectations. Gross *et al.* (1958) operationally defined this by first assessing in an interview what expectations a subject perceived as held for him or her by relevant others, and then assessing whether or not the subject believed they had the right to hold such expectations. Thus, an expectation perceived by a mother as held for her was said to be *legitimate* if it was mutually accepted by the mother and the relevant other, i.e., the mother accepted the relevant other's right to hold a given expectation. Perhaps a more descriptive term for the perceived legitimacy of expectations is the perceived reasonableness of demands.

As in the Gross *et al.* study, this reasonableness was ascertained by an interviewer who inquired of the subject:

DO YOU THINK:
Your children
Your husband
Your parents
Most other people you know

HAVE THE RIGHT TO EXPECT YOU TO:
Look after the kinds of friends your children have?
Impart respect for authority to your children?
Protect your children from dangers of the streets?
Involve your husband in the rearing of your children?

The information thus obtained was dichotomized so that if a mother perceived a relevant other as having the right to a given expectation, this was indicated as L+; whereas if she perceived the relevant other as not having that right, this was indicated as L-. If incompatible demands E'/E were perceived for an issue, then four different combinations of perceived legitimacy are theoretically possible: L+/L+, L+/L-, L-/L+, or L-/L-. For example, L+/L+ would mean that the mother perceived incompatible demands on her, both of which she also perceived as reasonable or legitimate (e.g., E from her parents and E' from her children).

Sanctions

Sanctions have been identified by Gross *et al.* (1958) as negative consequences conditional on how an individual behaves. These authors operationally defined external sanctions by asking the subject in an interview situation how a relevant other would react if he/she failed to meet the relevant other's expectations. Perceived sanctions thus were defined as the expected consequences if the other's demands were not met, with sanctions equivalent to negative consequences.

In order to assess the negative consequences attached to perceived demands, the interviewer asked the subject:

HOW WOULD: Your children
      Your husband
      Your parents
      Most other people you know

REACT IF YOU FAILED TO DO WHAT
THEY EXPECT OF YOU IN REFERENCE TO:
      Looking after the kinds of friends your children have?
      Imparting respect for authority to your children?
      Protecting your children from dangers of the streets?
      Involving your husband in the rearing of the children?

The information obtained was dichotomized so that if a mother perceived that failure to comply with a given expectation resulted in negative consequences from a relevant other, this was denoted as S-; whereas if she did not perceive negative consequences for non-compliance, this was indicated as S+. If incompatible demands (E'/E) were perceived, then four different combinations of sanctions are possible: S+/S+, S+/S-, S-/S+, or S-/S-. For example, S-/S- indicates that failure to comply with either incompatible expectation was perceived as resulting in negative sanctions.

Results

Mothers' perceptions of *expectations, legitimacy,* and *sanctions* were extremely homogeneous. For the great majority of cases, mothers perceived adults, such as members of their nuclear and extended family as well as friends, as *expecting them to behave along cultural norms.* Moreover, mothers felt strongly that these individuals *had a legitimate right* to expect this. Mothers also believed that these adult role definers would apply *negative consequences* if they failed to behave in a culturally appropriate fashion. The only instances of dissent, giving rise to role conflicts, were found when youngsters were perceived as expecting their mothers to behave in a fashion contrary to cultural expectations.

Role Conflicts

Role conflicts were defined as situations where incompatible role expectations for the mother were perceived by her as being held by two relevant others (role definers) in relation to a particular issue. Such expectations were assessed on the basis of data gathered in an interview. These included the expectations perceived as held by each subject's children, husband, parents, and relevant others in relation to the four different issue areas.

The patterns of compatible and incompatible expectations perceived by the mothers as held for them by each pair of role definers for each of four issues are presented in Tables I-IV. As these tables indicate, among the various role definers in the life context of the mother, incompatible expectations are most prevalent between children and husbands, children and parents, and children and others. Conflicting expectations seldom occur between husbands and parents, husbands and others, or parents and others. As these tables also show, there seems to be considerable agreement between the expectations perceived by the mother as held for her by adult role definers and her own self-report of the expectations she holds for herself.

It would appear then that role conflicts comprised of perceived incompatible expectations essentially occur between children and adults, including the mother herself. With *very high* regularity, adults agree with each other in expecting the mother to bring up her children (i.e., behave) in a fashion that is consistent with the Cuban cultural prescription as perceived by the investigators for the role of a Cuban mother. The bulk of the role conflicts identified occur when children are perceived as expecting from their mother behaviors which are in disagreement with culturally defined prescriptions for her role.

Exceptions to these findings occur in Issue D with respect to the involvement of husbands in the rearing of children. As Table IV indicates, when some mothers perceived their husbands as expecting not to be involved in the rearing of children—E'(h)—and simultaneously perceived other role definers as holding the opposite expectation—E(c), E(p), E(o)— then role conflicts occurred.

An apparent role conflict occurred in relation to Issue D in cases in which all role definers expected husbands to be involved in the rearing of children—E(c), E(h), E(p), E(o)—but mothers did not think it was necessary to involve these husbands actively—E'(m). Clinical impressions obtained during the interviews strongly suggest that the latter type of role conflict is more apparent than real. In these cases, husbands usually were involved and expected to continue to be involved with their children without opposition from the mother. As may be expected, in these cases mothers were quite satisfied with the level of husband involvement and, therefore, did not see a need to *further* involve their husbands. For this reason, care must be taken in interpreting the information presented in Table IV and subsequent summary tables since the incompatible expecta- tions between role definers who expect husbands to be involved in the children's upbringing and mothers who see no need to *further* involve them, are not a source of role conflicts for the mothers.

Table V summarizes the information in Tables I-IV. It presents the total number of instances in which compatible (no role conflict) and incompa- tible (role conflict situations) expectations were identified in each of the four content (issue) areas between each pair of role definers, including those between the mothers' own expectations and role definers. Table VI presents the proportion of expectations found to conflict between role definers and between mothers and role definers. These tables clarify further the results presented in Tables I-IV. As these tables indicate, substantial numbers of conflicts occur only between children and adults. When the expectations of children and adults are paired, pooling across issues, 52.4 percent of the cases involve incompatible expectations. In contrast, when the expectations of pairs of adults are compared across issues, only 10.8 percent involve conflicting expectations, a sizable

TABLE I

EXPECTATIONS FOR HER BEHAVIOR PERCEIVED BY THE MOTHER AS HELD BY PAIRS OF ROLE DEFINERS IN RELATION TO ISSUE A (LOOKING AFTER THE KIND OF FRIENDS HER CHILDREN HAVE) AND THE MOTHER'S REPORTED EXPECTATIONS FOR HERSELF IN RELATION TO ISSUE A

	E(c)	E'(c)	E(h)	E'(h)	E(p)	E'(p)	E(o)	E'(o)	E(m)	E'(m)
E(c)			44	0	44	0	41	1	45	0
E'(c)			59	3	60	2	51	7	62	0
E(c) + E'(c)			103	3	104	2	92	8	107	0
E(h)	44	59			103	1	90	9	105	0
E'(h)	0	3			3	1	3	0	4	0
E(h) + E'(h)	44	62			106	2	93	9	109	0
E(p)	44	60	103	3			91	9	106	0
E'(p)	0	2	1	1			1	0	2	0
E(p) + E'(p)	44	62	104	4			92	9	108	0
E(o)	41	51	90	3	91	1			93	0
E'(o)	1	7	9	0	9	0			9	0
E(o) + E'(o)	42	58	99	3	100	1			102	0
E(m)	45	62	105	4	106	2	93	9		
E'(m)	0	0	0	0	0	0	0	0		
E(m) + E'(m)	45	62	105	4	106	2	93	9		
Mean E	44	58	86	3	86	1	79	7	87	0
Mean E'	0	3	17	1	18	1	14	2	19	0
Mean E + E'	44	61	103	4	104	2	93	9	107	0

NOTES: Unprimed notations = expectations in accord with Cuban cultural norms.
Primed notations = expectations contrary to Cuban cultural norms.
Expectations perceived by the mother as held for her by:

E(c) = her children.
E(h) = her husband.
E(p) = her parents.
E(o) = most other people she knows.
E(m) = mother's self-reported expectations for herself.

TABLE II

EXPECTATIONS FOR HER BEHAVIOR PERCEIVED BY THE MOTHER AS HELD BY PAIRS OF ROLE DEFINERS IN RELATION TO ISSUE B (IMPARTING RESPECT FOR AUTHORITY TO HER CHILDREN) AND THE MOTHER'S EXPECTATIONS FOR HERSELF IN RELATION TO ISSUE B

	E(c)	E'(c)	E(h)	E'(h)	E(p)	E'(p)	E(o)	E'(o)	E(m)	E'(m)
E(c)			41	0	41	0	38	2	41	0
E'(c)			61	1	62	0	55	1	62	0
E(c) + E'(c)			102	1	103	0	93	3	103	0
E(h)	41	61			106	0	93	4	106	0
E'(h)	0	1			2	0	2	0	0	0
E(h) + E'(h)	41	62			108	0	95	4	106	0
E(p)	41	62	106	2			95	4	107	0
E'(p)	0	0	0	0			0	0	0	0
E(p) + E'(p)	41	62	106	2			95	4	107	0
E(o)	38	55	93	2	95	0			95	0
E'(o)	2	1	4	0	4	0			4	0
E(o) + E'(o)	40	56	97	2	99	0			99	0
E(m)	41	62	106	0	107	0	95	4		
E'(m)	0	0	0	0	0	0	0	0		
E(m) + E'(m)	41	62	106	0	107	0	95	4		
Mean E	40	60	87	1	87	0	80	4	87	0
Mean E'	1	1	16	0	17	0	15	0	16	0
Mean E + E'	41	61	103	1	104	0	95	4	103	0

NOTES: Unprimed notations = expectations in accord with Cuban cultural norms.
Primed notations = expectations contrary to Cuban cultural norms.
Expectations perceived by the mother as held for her by:

E(c) = her children.
E(h) = her husband.
E(p) = her parents.
E(o) = most other people she knows.
E(m) = mother's self-reported expectations for herself.

TABLE III

EXPECTATIONS FOR HER BEHAVIOR PERCEIVED BY THE MOTHER AS HELD BY PAIRS OF ROLE DEFINERS IN RELATION TO ISSUE C (PROTECTING HER CHILDREN FROM DANGERS OF THE STREETS) AND THE MOTHER'S REPORTED EXPECTATIONS FOR HERSELF IN RELATION TO ISSUE C

	E(c)	E'(c)	E(h)	E'(h)	E(p)	E'(p)	E(o)	E'(o)	E(m)	E'(m)
E(c)			39	0	38	0	36	0	39	0
E'(c)			59	4	63	1	52	3	61	2
E(c) + E'(c)			98	4	101	1	88	3	100	2
E(h)	39	59			101	0	88	2	99	2
E'(h)	0	4			5	0	3	1	5	0
E(h) + E'(h)	39	63			106	0	91	3	104	2
E(p)	38	63	101	5			90	3	102	2
E'(p)	0	1	0	0			0	0	1	0
E(p) + E'(p)	38	64	101	5			90	3	103	2
E(o)	36	52	88	3	90	0			89	1
E'(o)	0	3	2	1	3	0			3	0
E(o) + E'(o)	36	55	90	4	93	0			92	1
E(m)	39	61	99	5	101	1	89	3		
E'(m)	0	2	2	0	2	0	1	0		
E(m) + E'(m)	39	63	101	5	103	1	90	3		
Mean E	38	59	82	3	83	25	76	2	82	1
Mean E'	0	2	16	2	18	25	12	1	18	1
Mean E + E'	38	61	98	5	101	50	88	3	100	2

NOTES: Unprimed notations = expectations in accord with Cuban cultural norms.
Primed notations = expectations contrary to Cuban cultural norms.
Expectations perceived by the mother as held for her by:

E(c) = her children.
E(h) = her husband.
E(p) = her parents.
E(o) = most other people she knows.
E(m) = mother's self-reported expectations for herself.

TABLE IV

EXPECTATIONS FOR HER BEHAVIOR PERCEIVED BY THE MOTHER AS HELD BY PAIRS OF ROLE DEFINERS IN RELATION TO ISSUE D (GETTING HER HUSBAND MORE INVOLVED IN THE UPBRINGING OF THE CHILDREN) AND THE MOTHER'S REPORTED EXPECTATIONS FOR HERSELF IN RELATION TO ISSUE D

	E(c)	E'(c)	E(h)	E'(h)	E(p)	E'(p)	E(o)	E'(o)	E(m)	E'(m)
E(c)			57	19	67	7	56	12	48	25
E'(c)			15	8	21	2	16	4	12	10
E(c) + E'(c)			72	27	88	9	72	16	60	35
E(h)	57	15			67	5	54	8	39	28
E'(h)	19	8			20	4	18	6	18	8
E(h) + E'(h)	76	23			87	9	72	14	57	36
E(p)	67	21	67	20			71	7	52	31
E'(p)	7	2	5	4			2	5	4	4
E(p) + E'(p)	74	23	72	24			73	12	56	35
E(o)	56	16	54	18	71	2			45	25
E'(o)	12	4	8	6	7	5			7	6
E(o) + E'(o)	68	20	62	24	78	7			52	31
E(m)	48	12	39	18	52	4	45	7		
E'(m)	25	10	28	8	31	4	25	6		
E(m) + E'(m)	73	22	67	26	83	8	70	13		
Mean E	57	16	47	19	64	5	57	9	46	20
Mean E'	16	6	21	6	20	3	15	5	10	14
Mean E + E'	73	22	68	25	84	8	72	14	56	34

NOTES: Unprimed notations = expectations in accord with Cuban cultural norms.
Primed notations = expectations contrary to Cuban cultural norms.
Expectations perceived by the mother as held for her by:

E(c) = her children.
E(h) = her husband.
E(p) = her parents.
E(o) = most other people she knows.
E(m) = mother's self-reported expectations for herself.

TABLE V

NUMBER OF INSTANCES IN WHICH COMPATIBLE (C) AND INCOMPATIBLE (I) EXPECTATIONS WERE PERCEIVED BY THE MOTHERS AS BEING HELD FOR THEM BY EACH ROLE PAIR IN EACH ISSUEa

	ISSUE A		ISSUE B		ISSUE C		ISSUE D		MEAN		MEAN	
	Ib	Cc	I	C	I	C	I	C	I	C	I	C
Child/ Husband	59	47	61	42	59	43	34	65	53.3	49.3		
Child/ Parent	60	46	62	41	63	39	28	69	53.3	48.8	52.5	47.7
Child/ Other	52	48	57	39	52	39	28	60	47.3	46.5		
Child/ Mother	62	45	62	41	61	41	40	58	56.3	46.3		
Husband/ Parent	4	104	2	106	5	101	25	71	9.0	5.5		
Husband/ Other	12	90	6	93	5	89	26	60	12.3	83.0	11.8	89.3
Husband/ Mother	4	105	0	106	7	99	46	47	14.3	89.3		
Parent/ Other	10	91	4	95	3	90	9	76	6.5	88.0	8.3	90.4
Parent/ Mother	2	106	0	107	3	102	35	56	10.0	92.8		
Other/ Mother	9	93	4	95	4	89	32	51	12.3	82.0	12.3	82.0
Mean	27.4	77.5	25.8	76.5	26.1	73.2	30.3	61.3	27.4	72.2	27.4	72.2

a   See text for description of issues.

Ib   Number of instances in which *incompatible* expectations (role conflicts) were perceived by the mothers as being held for them by each pair of role definers.

Cc   Number of instances in which *compatible* expectations were perceived by the mothers as being held for them by each pair of role definers.

TABLE VI

**PERCENTAGE OF CONFLICTS TO TOTAL NUMBER OF EXPECTATIONS
CONTRASTED IN EACH PAIR OF ROLE DEFINERS AND
BETWEEN MOTHERS AND ROLE DEFINERS**

	ISSUE A %	ISSUE B %	ISSUE C %	ISSUE D %	MEAN %	MEAN %
Child/ Husband	55.6	59.2	57.8	34.3	51.7	
Child/ Parent	56.6	60.2	61.8	28.9	51.9	52.4
Child/ Other	52.0	59.4	57.1	31.8	50.8	
Child/ Mother	57.9	60.2	59.8	40.8	54.7	
Husband/ Parent	3.7	1.9	4.7	26.0	9.1	
Husband/ Other	11.8	6.1	5.3	30.2	13.4	11.7
Husband/ Mother	3.7	0.0	6.6	49.5	15.0	
Parent/ Other	9.9	4.0	3.2	10.6	6.9	8.4
Parent/ Mother	1.9	0.0	2.9	38.5	10.8	
Other/ Mother	8.1	4.0	4.3	38.6	13.8	13.8
Mean	26.1	25.1	26.4	32.9	27.7	27.7

number of which represent the mock role conflicts identified in Issue D between mothers and role definers, rather than real role conflicts resulting from conflicting demands of others upon the mother.

Clinical impressions obtained during research interviews suggest strongly that the expectations perceived from children, husbands, and parents are substantially more relevant to the mothers than the expectations perceived as held by "most other people you know." By the same token, the negative sanctions associated with the expectations of the children, husband, and parents are perceived by the mothers as more tangible and substantially stronger than those perceived from "other people." All of the interviewers reported that the mothers definitely gave more weight to their children's, husbands', and parents' wishes than to those of "other people." As perhaps should have been foreseen, in the tightly knit Cuban families expectations of close family members are more important to the mother than the expectations of other individuals outside the family nucleus; and the sanctions controlled by these family members are, at least around family issues, much stronger than those controlled by others outside the family nucleus.

These clinical findings suggest that for the mothers in this study, the expectations they perceive as held for them by "most other people you know" are of relatively little importance. Based on these findings, the patterns of legitimacy and sanctions attached to perceived expectations are presented in the subsequent sections of this paper only as a function of the expectations identified as held by children, husbands, and parents.

Thus, in the role conflict situations identified in Issues A, B, and C, essentially only one pattern of expectations was observed (Tables I, II, and III), in that role conflicts occurred only when adults were perceived as holding expectations in accord with Cuban cultural norms and children were perceived as holding counter-cultural expectations. Therefore, for Issues A, B, and C, "cultural expectations" are synonymous with "adults' expectations," and "counter-cultural expectations" are synonymous with "children's expectations." For Issue D (Table IV), however, more variability was observed. On this issue some adults and some children were perceived as holding cultural and some counter-cultural expectations.

Sources of Role Conflicts

Two pairs of role definers, children/husbands and children/parents, were singled out as important sources of role conflicts in Cuban mothers. For any given mother, role conflicts could be identified whose source was either one or both pairs of role definers within each of the issue areas under investigation. Table VII contrasts the patterns of expectations identified for both pairs of role definers in each of the four issues assessed. As can be seen from this table, in 83 percent of the cases in which incompatible expectations were perceived between one pair of these role definers, it was perceived also for the second pair. Essentially then, the role conflicts observed reduce to differences in child/adult expectations perceived by the mother.

Legitimacy

Table VIII presents the legitimacy attached by the mothers to the various expectations perceived as held for them by their children, husbands, and parents on each of the four issues. Nearly all of the

TABLE VII

CONTRASTING PATTERNS OF PERCEIVED EXPECTATIONS FOR TWO PAIRS OF ROLE DEFINERS ON FOUR ISSUES

	ISSUE A Child/Parent					ISSUE B Child/Parent		
	E/E	E'/E	E'/E'			E/E	E'/E	E'/E'
	E/E	43	1	0		E/E	41	0	0
Child/	E'/E	0	58	2	Child/	E'/E	0	60	1
Husband	E'/E'	0	1	1	Husband	E'/E'	0	0	0

	ISSUE C Child/Parent					ISSUE D Child-Parent Pair		
	E/E	E'/E	E'/E'			E/E	E'/E	E'/E'
	E/E	38	0	0	Child-	E/E	50	5	0
Child/	E'/E	0	59	4	Husband	E'/E	14	16	0
Husband	E'/E'	0	0	0	Pair	E'/E'	0	6	2

	MEAN FOR ISSUES A, B, & C Child/Parent					MEAN FOR ALL ISSUES Child-Parent Pair		
	E/E	E'/E	E'/E'			E/E	E'/E	E'/E'
	E/E	41	0	0	Child-	E/E	43	2	0
Child/	E'/E	0	59	2	Husband	E'/E	4	48	2
Husband	E'/E'	0	0	0	Pair	E'/E'	0	2	1

NOTES:

E/E   Mother perceives compatible expectations for her behavior from both role definers which are compatible with Cuban cultural norms.

E'/E'   Mother perceives compatible expectations for her behavior from role definers, but these are contrary to Cuban cultural norms.

E'/E   Mother perceives incompatible expectations for her behavior: either the child or the adult role definer is perceived as expecting the mother to behave contrary to Cuban cultural norms and the remaining role definer is perceived as expecting the mother to behave in accordance with Cuban cultural norms. In Issues A, B, and C, E' always refers to children, and E always refers to adults.

TABLE VIII

EXPECTATIONS AND CORRESPONDING LEGITIMACY VALUES PERCEIVED BY MOTHERS AS HELD FOR THEM BY THEIR CHILDREN, HUSBANDS, AND PARENTS IN EACH OF FOUR ISSUES[a]

		ISSUE A			ISSUE B			ISSUE C			ISSUE D			MEAN FOR ALL ISSUES		
		L+	L-	(L+)+(L-)	L+	L-	(L+)+(L-)	L+	L-	(L+)+(L-)	L+	L-	(L+)+(L-)	L+	L-	(L+)+(L-)
Children	E	41	1	42	37	0	37	39	9	48	80	0	80	49	0	49
	E'	2	58	60	1	61	62	1	59	60	2	19	21	2	49	51
	E+E'	43	59	102	38	61	99	40	68	108	82	19	101	51	49	100
Husband	E	104	1	105	106	0	106	100	1	101	75	0	75	96	1	97
	E'	0	3	3	0	1	1	2	2	4	0	26	26	1	8	9
	E+E'	104	4	108	106	1	107	102	3	105	75	26	101	97	9	106
Parents	E	105	1	106	103	3	106	104	1	105	89	0	89	100	1	101
	E'	0	1	1	0	0	0	0	0	0	2	5	7	1	2	3
	E+E'	105	2	107	103	3	106	104	1	105	91	5	96	101	3	104
Mean for all Role Definers	E	83	1	84	82	1	83	81	1	82	81	0	81	82	1	83
	E'	1	21	22	0	21	21	1	20	21	1	17	18	1	20	21
	E+E'	84	22	106	82	22	104	82	21	103	82	17	99	83	21	104

NOTES:

a See text for description of issues.

E (Unprimed) = Expectations perceived by the mother as held by relevant others for her proper behavior in accordance with cultural norms.

E' (Primed) = Expectations perceived by the mother as held by relevant others for her behavior as contrary to cultural norms.

L+ = Expectations of others are perceived as legitimate and reasonable by the mother.

L- = Expectations of others are perceived as illegitimate or unreasonable by the mother.

58

mothers perceived their children, husbands, and parents as having a legitimate right to hold expectations when these are in accord with Cuban cultural norms. Just as consistently, mothers refused to endorse counter-cultural expectations as legitimate. These findings suggest that the perceived legitimacy of expectations depends much more on their relation to the Cuban culture than on who is perceived as holding the expectation. Although variability in legitimacy patterns had been expected, little was observed in this study. In fact, in 98 percent of the role conflict situations, mothers endorsed the legitimate right of role definers to expect them to behave in accord with Cuban values and refused to endorse counter-cultural expectations as legitimate, regardless of who held them.

Sanctions

Table IX presents the sanctions attached by the mothers to the various expectations perceived as held for them by their children, husbands, and parents on each of the four issues. Most mothers who perceived expectations to behave in accord with Cuban cultural norms also perceived negative consequences for failing to behave thus, and this was particularly true for the expectations perceived as being held for them by their parents and husbands. However, when mothers perceived expectations requiring them to behave contrary to Cuban norms, then negative consequences were perceived as frequently as no consequences for failing to comply with these expectations.

Table X presents the patterns of sanctions perceived by the mothers in role conflict situations based on incompatible expectations between children and husbands and between children and parents. Ninety-seven percent of the sanction patterns observed in role conflict situations were of two types. In one of the prevalent patterns—(S+/S-)—the mothers perceived negative consequences for failing to comply with expectations that they behave in accord with Cuban cultural norms. In the other prevalent pattern of sanctions observed—(S-/S-)—the mothers perceived negative consequences both for failing to comply with expectations in the cultural direction and for failing to comply with expectations in the counter-cultural direction.

Discussion

Homogeneity of the Population

It has been reported frequently in the literature that a pervasive characteristic of Hispanic groups is the homogeneity of values and beliefs within their cultures, and particularly in reference to the definitions of family roles and family structures (e.g., Padilla and Ruiz, 1973; Padilla and Aranda, 1974). Consistent with these earlier findings, the mothers in the study reported here perceived with great regularity certain sets of expectations, legitimacies, and sanctions. Essentially only one kind of role conflict situation was found for the first three issues (A, B, and C), those which concerned the mothers' expected behaviors toward their children. In these issues, adults were perceived by the mothers as expecting them to comply with culturally sanctioned expectations pertaining to their maternal role. Thus, there was very high agreement among all adult role definers and the mothers as to the nature of the responsibilities of a Cuban mother. On these same issues, since adult role definers held culturally

TABLE IX

MOTHERS' PERCEIVED EXPECTATIONS AND CORRESPONDING SANCTIONS FOR NON-COMPLIANCE[a]

	ISSUE A			ISSUE B			ISSUE C			ISSUE D			MEAN FOR ALL ISSUES		
	S+	S-	(S+)+(S-)	S+	S-	(S+)+(S-)	S+	S-	(S+)+(S-)	S+	S-	(S+)+(S-)	S+	S-	(S+)+(S-)
Children															
E	14	31	45	14	27	41	7	32	39	7	73	80	11	41	52
E'	34	28	62	35	27	62	31	33	64	7	18	25	27	27	54
E+E'	48	59	107	49	54	103	38	65	103	14	91	105	38	68	106
Husband															
E	5	100	105	5	102	107	3	99	102	5	71	76	5	93	98
E'	2	2	4		1	1	3	3	6	20	7	27	6	3	9
E+E'	7	102	109	5	103	108	6	102	108	25	78	103	11	96	107
Parents															
E	0	106	106	0	108	108	0	107	107	2	89	91	1	103	104
E'	2	1	3	0	0	0	0	0	1	5	4	9	2	1	3
E+E'	2	107	109	0	108	108	1	107	108	7	93	100	3	104	107
Mean for all Role Definers															
E	6	79	85	6	79	85	3	79	82	5	77	82	5	79	84
E'	13	10	23	12	9	21	12	12	24	11	10	21	12	10	22
E+E'	19	89	108	18	88	106	15	91	106	16	87	103	17	89	106

NOTES:

a= See text for description of issues.

E (Unprimed) = Expectations perceived by the mother as held by relevant others for her proper behavior in accordance with cultural norms.

E' (Primed) = Expectations perceived by the mother as held by relevant others for her behavior as contrary to cultural norms.

S+ = No consequences are perceived by the mother for failing to comply with expectations.

S- = Negative consequences are perceived by the mother for failing to comply with expectations.

TABLE X

PATTERNS OF SANCTIONS PERCEIVED IN ROLE CONFLICT SITUATIONS

E'/E	ISSUE A				ISSUE B				ISSUE C				ISSUE D			
	S+/S+	S-/S+	S+/S-	S-/S-	S+/S+	S-/S+	S+/S-	S-/S-	S+/S+	S-/S+	S+/S-	S-/S-	S+/S+	S-/S+	S+/S-	S-/S-
Child/ Husband	0	0	32	28	0	0	35	26	0	0	30	33	3	0	15	16
Child/ Parent	1	3	33	23	1	2	34	23	1	2	28	28	1	0	9	11
Percent per Issue	1	3	54	43	1	2	56	40	1	2	48	50	7	0	44	48

NOTES:

E= Expectations perceived for mother's behavior as in accordance with Cuban cultural norms.

E'= Expectations perceived for mother's behavior contrary to Cuban cultural norms.

S+/S+= No consequences are perceived for non-compliance with E' or E.

S-/S+= Negative consequences are perceived for non-compliance with E' and no consequences are perceived for non-compliance with E.

S+/S-= No consequences are perceived for non-compliance with E', and negative consequences are perceived for non-compliance with E.

S-/S-= Negative consequences are perceived for non-compliance with E' and E.

Issues A, B, and C: E' conflicts are virtually always perceived as being held by children.

consistent expectations for mothers, no role conflict existed. But when the children disagreed with these role prescriptions, then and only then did role conflicts occur.

Mothers' perceptions of legitimacy were extremely consistent. The same pattern of legitimacy was observed in 96 percent of all role conflict situations. *The perceived legitimacy* or *reasonableness of demands* attached to perceived expectations *was strongly related to the cultural appropriateness of the expectations.* Almost without exception, if a role definer expected the culturally defined behavior from the mother, then the expectation was perceived as legitimate and reasonable. Just as consistently, mothers refused to endorse the right of role definers to hold counter-cultural expectations. In role conflict situations around A, B, and C, adults were virtually always perceived as expecting the culturally defined behaviors, and children as expecting the opposite. Consequently, in role conflict situations around these issues, the expectations of adults were perceived as legitimate and the expectations of children were perceived as illegitimate.

With regard to sanctions, two different patterns occurred in role conflict situations. Mothers nearly always perceived negative consequences for failing to comply with expectations in the cultural direction. In many cases of role conflict, mothers perceived no sanctions for failing to comply with counter-cultural expectations, but in some cases negative sanctions were also perceived for non-compliance with them.

The expectations perceived by the mothers as held for them by adult role definers document once more the homogeneity of role definitions that exist in Latin cultures and especially around the role of the mother. However, in over 50 percent of the cases, the expectations perceived by the mothers as held for them by their children were contrary to cultural norms, illustrating the intergenerational conflicts of expectations and role definitions that arise in many immigrant families. In immigrant Cuban families these intergenerational differences become exacerbated and tend to become a major source of family disruption (Scopetta, King, and Szapocznik, 1975; Szapocznik et al., 1978a).

The conflicts in expectations and role definitions experienced by these mothers are a source of role stress. Moreover, the disruptive effect on the family of these incompatible demands are also a source of stress for the mother who sees herself as having failed both in communicating cultural norms to her children and in maintaining and preserving the unity of the family. Both of these tasks are seen in the Cuban culture as role-specific to the mother.

These interpretations of the data should be taken cautiously, however, since the sample in this study was not meant to be representative of the Cuban immigrant population as a whole. In fact, the sample includes a large proportion of mothers who are *a priori* known to be from families with psycho-social problems (e.g., depressed mothers or "acting out" adolescents). Nevertheless, the findings illustrate one possible source of disruption in these families.

Clinical Implications of Homogeneity

Cuban women, like most other Latin women, have been raised in cultural contexts which are highly consistent in their definition of roles. In Cuba before 1959, for example, there was considerable agreement among

adults, children, and socio-cultural institutions regarding the responsibilities of, and the expectations for, the role of a mother. In contrast, the
United States today is a variegated nation with little agreement on role
definitions. For this reason, if a Cuban mother living in the United States in
the 1970s depends on the role definitions that others hold for her in order
to determine her own responsibilities as a mother, she would become
confused by the many definitions. Rather, because of the heterogeneity of role definitions in this country, a mother here must review the
available definitions and decide what she is to expect of herself.

When a Cuban mother, after having been prepared to live in a socio-
cultural context that presents a single definition of her responsibilities, is
propelled by her children's dissent into a maternal role with conflicting
expectations, she either becomes confused or must develop her own
definitions of her role as a mother. The latter alternative requires a
modicum of flexibility to integrate successfully the variety of role demands
on the mother. Those mothers who remain in a world of absolutes and are
least flexible in making adjustments confront the greatest personal and
familial difficulties (Szapocznik et al., 1978c).

Drug Usage (Sedatives and Tranquilizers)
Among Cuban Mothers in Conflict

The data presented in this paper were obtained as part of a study
investigating the relationship between drug use and role conflicts in
Cuban mothers. Although the data on drug use are presented elsewhere, it
is of heuristic value to briefly discuss here the relationship between role
conflicts and drug usage by these mothers since it helps to bring into
perspective the findings presented in this paper. Analyses of drug usage
among the 110 Cuban mothers in this study reveal that drug-using
mothers were less acculturated, presented more neurotic personality
profiles as measured by Cattell's 16 PF* (Cattell, Eber, and Tatsicoka,
1970), and perceived a greater number of role conflicts. Moreover, the
greatest use of sedatives and tranquilizers was found among those
mothers who (1) as a personality characteristic tended to view things in
"black and white," that is, in terms of absolutes, and (2) simultaneously
were exposed to role conflicts in which they were threatened by negative
sanctions from both directions (i.e., perceived negative sanctions for
failing to behave in the way that adults expected of them as well as for
failing to behave in the way that their children expected).

It should be noted that if drug-using mothers reported more role
conflicts, this could result from their biased perception of conflict or,
alternatively, from real conflict to which they are exposed. Data obtained
by objective ratings of interviewers suggest that drug-using mothers were
actually exposed to more serious and real family and environmental
conflicts than mothers who did not use drugs.

Family and role conflicts do not appear randomly. Rather, some
personality characteristics of mothers and some relationship patterns in
families seem to attract more than their random share of conflicts. Our
findings (Szapocznik, 1976) suggest that intra-family intergenerational
conflicts are significantly more prevalent among mothers who are too
strict in their views—i.e., perceive ideas, behaviors, and values in absolute
terms—and among families in which the father may not be a full partner in

---

*Spanish version.

raising the children. Clearly, a major source of stress results from the youngsters' Americanization (Szapocznik *et al.,* 1978b). But when mothers are too absolute in their views, they may not be able to facilitate a smooth and natural transition to greater, although disciplined, independence in their maturing adolescents. (Note that it is a typical development of adolescence to strive for greater independence.) On the other hand, rebelling adolescents can be extremely difficult to handle and unless both mother and father are parenting together and devoting considerable attention to their youngsters, the family may not achieve the discipline necessary to permit this greater, although disciplined, independence.

Mothers experiencing the most stress, confronted with the most role conflicts, and perhaps abusing the most medicinal drugs may be described as perfectionists. They believe that families should function ideally, and they are convinced that their own ideals for their family are realistic. Falling short of these goals creates frustration, perhaps because these mothers have not developed the capability of adjusting to changing situations. For these perfectionist mothers, the transitional period, represented by migration/acculturation and exacerbated by the rapid changes of adolescence, represents an unmanageable task of readjustment for which medicinal drug use may be one coping solution. Further research on the perfectionist mother and on effective therapeutic assistance for these mothers and their families is recommended.

REFERENCES

Al-Issa, I. Culture and symptoms. *In* C.G. Costello (ed.), *Symptoms of Psychopathology: A Handbook.* New York: John Wiley and Sons, 1970.

Berry, J.W. and Annis, R. Acculturative stress: the role of ecology, culture, and differentiation *Journal of Cross-Cultural Psychology,* 1974, 5(4), 382-406.

Cattell, R.B.; Eber, H.W.; and Tatsicoka, M.M. *Handbook of the Sixteen Personality Factor Questionnaire.* Champaign, Illinois: Institute for Personality and Ability Testing, 1970.

Gerth, H. and Mills, C.W. *Character and Social Structure.* New York: Harcourt and Brace, 1953.

Goldsen, R.K.; Mills, C.W.; and Senior, C. *The Puerto Rican Journey.* New York: Harper Brothers, 1972.

Gross, N.; McEacher, A.W.; and Mason, W.S. *Exploration in Role Analysis.* New York: John Wiley and Sons, 1958.

_____ Role conflict and its resolution. *In* B.J. Biddle and E.J. Thomas (eds.), *Role Theory: Concepts and Research.* New York: John Wiley and Sons, 1966.

Hass, J.E. *Role Conception and Group Consensus.* Research Monograph No. 117. Columbus: Ohio State University, 1964.

Hollingshead, A.B. *Two Factor Index of Social Position.* New Haven, Connecticut: A.B. Hollingshead, 1957.

Kelly, R. Mental illness in the Maori population of New Zealand. *Acta Psychiatrica Scandinava,* 1973, 49, 722-34.

Ladner, R.; Page, W.F.; and Lee, M.L. Ethnic and sex effects on emergency ward utilization for drug-related problems. *Journal of Health and Social Behavior,* 1975, 16, 315-25.

Mezey, A.G. Psychiatric aspects of human migrations. *International Journal of Social Psychiatry,* 1960, 5(4), 245-60.

Padilla, A.M. and Aranda, P. *Latino Mental Health: Bibliography and Abstracts.* DHEW Publication No. (HSM) 73-9144. Washington, D.C.: Government Printing Office, 1974.

Padilla, A.M. and Ruiz, R.A. *Latino Mental Health: A Review of the Literature.* DHEW Publication No. (HSM) 73-9143. Washington, D.C.: Government Printing Office, 1973.

Parsons, T. *The Social System.* New York: Free Press, 1951.

Penalosa, F. Mexican family roles. *Journal of Marriage and the Family,* 1968, *30,* 680-89.

Sarbin, T.R. and Allen, V.L. Role theory. *In* G. Lindsey and E. Aronson, *Handbook of Social Psychology,* Vol. I. Reading, Massachusetts: Addison-Wesley, 1968.

Scopetta, Mercedes A. and Alegre, C.A. Clinical issues in psychotherapy research with Latins. Paper presented at the Second National Conference on Drug Abuse, New Orleans, Louisiana, 1976.

Scopetta, Mercedes A.; King, Olga E.; and Szapocznik, J. Relationship of acculturation, incidence of drug abuse, and effective treatment for Cuban Americans. Report to the National Institute on Drug Abuse, Rockville, Maryland, for research contract #271-75-4136, July 1975.

Spiegel, J. Changing values and family conflict in a time of political disorders. Paper presented at the Tenth Anniversary Conference, New York Family Institute, New York, New York, 1970.

Szapocznik, J. Role conflict resolution in Cuban mothers. Doctoral dissertation, University of Miami (Florida), Coral Gables, 1976. Available from University Microfilms, P.O. Box 1764, Ann Arbor, Michigan 48106 (refer to publication #77-21, 898).

Szapocznik, J.; Scopetta, Mercedes A.; and King, Olga E. Theory and practice in matching treatment to the special characteristics and problems of Cuban immigrants. *Journal of Community Psychology,* 1978a, *6,* 112-122.

Szapocznik, J.; Scopetta, Mercedes A.; Kurtines, W.; and Aranalde, M.A. Theory and measurement of acculturation. *Interamerican Journal of Psychology,* in press, 1978b.

Szapocznik, J.; Scopetta, Mercedes A.; and Tillman, W. What changes, what stays the same, and what affects acculturative change? *In* J. Szapocznik and Maria Cristina Herrera, *Cuban Americans: Acculturation, Adjustment, and the Family.* Washington, D.C.: COSSMHO— The National Coalition of Hispanic Mental Health and Human Services Organizations, 1978c.

DEPENDENT NEEDY FAMILIES OF SAN JUAN, PUERTO RICO

Rosa C. Marin

This paper is based on three studies undertaken by the Graduate School of Social Work of the University of Puerto Rico (Acosta *et al.*, 1961; Marin, 1968; and Banuchi de Abreu *et al.*, 1970). These studies involved about 240 families (including approximately 1,440 individuals of varying ages) who lived in San Juan, Puerto Rico, during the period from 1961 to 1970. These families had been receiving social services continuously for five or more years from public welfare agencies of the Commonwealth and were considered by these agencies as indigent.

According to the 1970 census for Puerto Rico, 46 percent of the families in San Juan were indigent—that is, lived below the poverty level (U.S. Bureau of the Census, 1973). This means that families consisting of two members had an annual income of less than $2,364; those with three members, less than $2,905; those with four, less than $3,721; those with five, less than $4,386; those with six, less than $4,921; and those with seven or more, less than $6,034. These figures fluctuated according to the family's place of residence (urban or rural), the age of the head of household (65 and older, or less than 65), and the sex of the head of household (if the head of household was male, the range in income was higher). With regard to the number of indigent families, San Juan compared favorably with Ponce and Mayaguez inasmuch as in these latter cities, the number of indigent families was increasingly greater than 58 percent of the total.

What were the characteristics of the dependent families involved in the three studies? If I had to describe them on the basis of only one trait, I would characterize them as generous. In more technical terminology, their propensity to share inversely correlated with their earnings. It is well known that we all tend to describe things, people, and events within our own particular frame of reference, giving emphasis to the characteristics we consider most important or pertinent to our study of the situation. I give emphasis to the *vulnerability* or unusual hazards faced by the families I am attempting to describe. Families in the three studies have been called by a close colleague of mine as "the poorest of the poor." That is, with regard to the level of poverty defined by demographers and economists, these families are found on the lowest extreme end of the income earning scale. Herein lies part of their problem. In Puerto Rico I have heard astounding comments from eminent individuals in politics, economics, and finance who assert that "poor people do not exist on the island, but rather idle and shiftless people." I wish to underscore the fact that poverty (associated with low economic means), although prevalent among the families studied, is not their predominant trait. These families reflect the impact of a concatenation of factors that, in and of themselves, have a greater importance than does the absence or limited availability of economic means, the principal characteristic so often associated with this population. With this particular emphasis or frame of reference, let us consider selected characteristics of these families that emerged in the course of the study effort.

Summary of Family Characteristics

The families studied were defined as including "the presence of at least one minor, together with an adult related to the minor by blood, marriage, or affinity; in addition, the adult felt responsible for the behavior of the minor, and both the adult and the minor lived together under the same roof" (Marin, 1963).

With regard to family composition, there were 10 variations or types:

TYPES	PERCENT OF TOTAL
Married couple with children	31
Single parent (mother) with children	23
Single parent (mother) with children and other relatives	17.5
Married couple with children and other relatives	15
Single parent (father) with children	4
Married couple without children and with other relatives	3
Single parent (mother) with children and with other non-relative persons	2.5
Woman with parents	2
Single parent (father) with children and other relatives	1
Single parent (father and/or mother) with children in institutions	1

These ten types can be further grouped as follows:

CATEGORIES	PERCENT OF TOTAL
Married couple with or without children and other relatives	49

Truncated Family Nucleus

Single parent (mother) with children and other persons	43
Single parent (father) with children and others	5
Single parent (mother) with or without children in institutions and other relatives	3

The majority of the families (42 percent) lived in public housing, while 37.5 percent lived in the slums and the remainder in private residential areas within the city. Three out of every five families were tenants and paid a median monthly rent of $12.71.

The monthly income of these families—the median average—was $123, or $1,476 a year with a range of monthly income from $0 to $474. Per capita monthly income was $20.75.

Sources of family income were:

Private employment 38
Public assistance 37.5
Self-employment 26
Private economic assistance 22
Government employment 20
Social Security 16

In 52 percent of the families there was more than one source of income.

On the average, each family consisted of six members, four of them minors.

The majority of the heads of households (57 percent) were either illiterate or functionally illiterate. Only about 22.5 percent had received any education between grades seven and 14. The families were constituted mainly of women (51 percent) and minors or young children (67 percent).

The prevalence of long-term illnesses among these families was unusually high and affected 87 percent of the study sample. Within this group, two out of every five families had one or more members who had been the victim of an accident on the job, in the street, around the house, or involving a motor vehicle. In three out of every ten families there was an individual who was mentally ill. In 57.5 percent of the families one or more members were mentally retarded according to evidence derived from psychological tests administered during the studies.** In one out of every four families, one or more members had been convicted of serious crimes.

Desertion was more frequent among women than among men. Whereas one out of every four husbands had left the home at some point, one out of every three wives had done so. Among families where the partners were still together, 43 percent were legally married, 38 percent were living together by mutual agreement, and 17 percent were living in concubinage (meaning that one or both were legally married, but not to each other).

The majority of the heads of households had been born and raised outside of the metropolitan area of San Juan, but had migrated to the capital in search of greater income, educational, and health opportunities.

Each of the families identified the most serious community problems affecting its members. Problem areas cited were:

Presence of vermin and rodents
Excessive noise
Defective sewer drainage and standing pools of untreated sewage
Dirty streets and inadequate garbage collection
Drug addiction and illicit trafficking in drugs
Prostitution
Lack of medical facilities
Contagious or communicable diseases
Lack of pharmacies, schools, and grocery stores

Nevertheless, 56 percent of the families were satisfied with their

---

*Computation with duplication.

**The psychologist serving as consultant in this effort was Francisco Umpierre who interviewed 109 individuals, 91 of them minors or young children.

neighborhood, despite the fact that, in general, they did not maintain adequate contact with their neighbors—that is, they had not met them personally and did not know their names.

Family functioning was examined in seven areas: (1) intra-family relations, (2) individual behaviors and adaption, (3) financial and economic practices, (4) health problems and practices, (5) child rearing patterns, (6) social activities, and (7) housekeeping practices. In the beginning, all the families had problems in these seven areas, but at the end of two and one-half years of treatment and social intervention in the process by social workers associated with the project, one out of every three families was functioning in a satisfactory manner, and the remaining families (with the exception of about 10 percent) improved notably.

A survey of the attitudes and aspirations of the heads of families was undertaken as part of the study effort, and the findings proved to be somewhat disquieting. According to the psychological measures administered, family heads felt that they did not derive much satisfaction from personal attempts to overcome obstacles in life; consequently, their motivation for achievement and their disposition to succeed in situations requiring an evaluation of their performance according to a pre-established norm of excellence were quite low—only about three percent expressed a desire to achieve.* On the other hand, their motivation for power—that is, control of the behavior of others—was quite high: this feeling was expressed by three out of every four heads of households. The third motivational variable measured was affiliation—the propensity to give and receive affection—which was characteristic of only 22 percent of the heads of households who were queried on the matter.

Other opinions tapped revealed that three out of every 10 heads of households believed that a woman should not work outside the home for pay. Aspirations held by these families for their daughters were associated, first and foremost, with job opportunities in office-type positions, and, as a second choice, teaching careers. Aspirations for male children underscored employment as plumbers or carpenters as a first choice, and employment as factory workers or sales personnel in department stores as a second choice.

A common tendency among young children in these families was to fear one or both parents. Nevertheless, if they faced some problem or difficulty, the children consulted their mother or both parents and sought advice as to what to do and also shared the events of the day with them. School attendance among the children was sporadic. Absenteeism was largely attributed to illness, the fact that the child did not understand what was being taught, or the fact that the family lacked money to buy appropriate school clothing for the child. In about 21 percent of the families, there were children who had been brought before juvenile delinquency authorities. In applying Glueck's Social Prediction Scale to these youngsters, a 73 percent validity response for male juvenile delinquents was obtained as well as a 75 percent validity response for non-delinquent boys; the validity response among delinquent and non-delinquent girls reached 100 percent (Seplowin, 1960).

With regard to the sexual behavior of their children, the families studied appeared to be strict on the subject for both sons and daughters. They indicated that they neither permitted their adolescent daughters to go out

---

*Selected cards from the *Thematic Apperception Test* were used for this purpose.

on dates alone nor encouraged their sons to engage in sexual relations.

With regard to taking personal property belonging to another, study findings showed that 98 percent of the families living in public housing and 88.5 percent of those living in slums would require their children to return to its rightful owner any money obtained in an illegal manner. This particular attribute was voiced primarily by those classified as being illiterate. At the same time, 93 percent of the families declared that they did not support the belief that "the most important thing is to earn money, irrespective of the means."

A "good" husband, according to the women interviewed, was a man who "took full responsibility for household expenses and slept only with his wife."

It is worthwhile reiterating the importance given by these families to home ownership or the outright purchase of a home they could call their own. Families were asked what they would do if they won $15,000 from the lottery. Eighty-eight percent said they would either buy a house or purchase the lot where they currently resided, or they would enlarge the house where they now lived if it were their own. Others said they would buy a farm, pay off their debts, buy a small business, purchase a taxicab company, or contribute some support to charitable institutions and agencies.

Needy families taking part in the studies had been recipients of public welfare from the Puerto Rican social welfare system for an average period of nine and one-half years, and almost half of them had service records from the welfare agencies spanning a period of 10 to 19 consecutive years. In addition to these services, 120 families in the experimental group in one study had received services from 47 public and 28 private agencies, resulting in a grand total of 75 different agencies involved in meeting their needs. The staff that worked with these families had recruited a total of 154 volunteers who, in addition to meeting material needs not provided for by the agencies involved (such as dental care), nurtured a personal relationship which stimulated and maintained the interest of these families in their own rehabilitation.

To summarize, the etiological factors that gave rise to the urgent needs revealed in studies of these families point to the following specific circumstances:

1. The father was absent in 40 percent of the families as a result of death, prolonged hospitalization, imprisonment, migration to the continental United States, or desertion.
2. In 33 percent of the families there were "inadequate" mothers (i.e., mothers deriving income from sexual activity), uneducated parents, or parents who lacked adequate vocational skills.
3. In 24 percent of the cases, parents were physically or mentally disabled, e.g., they suffered from mental illness, including chronic alcoholism, or from advanced tuberculosis.

As is well known, Oscar Lewis (1966) advanced the hypothesis that indigent families possessed certain values and behaved in accord with specific norms: (1) a behavior pattern oriented toward the present—the "now"; (2) opportunism; (3) irrational use of money; (4) matriarchism; (5) instability of the family nucleus; and (6) male chauvinism or *machismo*. However, the Puerto Rican anthropologist, Professor Eduardo Seda

Bonilla, disagrees with the assumption of Lewis on the basis of carefully prepared individual case studies on 120 families involved in the study effort (Marin, 1967). According to Dr. Seda Bonilla, these indigent families are at best characterized by their lack of consensus and a propensity to suffer cultural erosion or "deculturalization."

Conclusion

Overall, there are five common traits in the family conditions described in this paper:

1. The existence of numerous families headed principally by a woman because the male parent was absent from the home due to death, prolonged illness, imprisonment, or desertion.

2. The prevalence of a low educational level among all members of the household which can best be described as illiteracy, including functional illiteracy.

3. The precarious health status of all family members due to poor nutrition, failure to seek medical care, failure to receive the necessary immunizations, a tendency toward having accidents, and continuous tension perpetuated by a sustained crisis setting threatening the mental health of all household members.

4. Problems in socialization of the young due to the absence of a mother figure and the failure to provide substitute child care or due to mental retardation and/or other physical and mental disabilities in the mother figure.

5. Absence of adult models in the home who can provide guidance and orientation and teach necessary skills to the young.

On the basis of such knowledge, social welfare agencies are in a better position to work to prevent the occurrence of dependent needy families and to help alleviate critical problems that such existing families face. The experience gained from these studies can help these agencies develop and carry out concrete preventive and therapeutic plans.

There is an optimistic note on which I would like to conclude, one that should serve as a stimulus to those working to help dependent families in need. Findings indicate that since the original project ended, the rehabilitated indigent families are continuing to improve their life conditions and have achieved notable improvement in the various areas of daily functioning. This progress should inspire directors and staff of human service agencies to persevere in their efforts on behalf of the poor.

REFERENCES

Acosta, Esperanza *et al*. *Recipiendarios de los servicios de bienestar del niño por cinco años consecutivos o más* (Recipients of child social welfare services for five or more consecutive years). University of Puerto Rico, Graduate School of Social Work, May 1961.

Banuchi de Abreu, Carmen Asia *et al*. *Estudio sobre familias atendidas en el Centro de Tratamiento Integral para la Familia* (Study on families served by the Comprehensive Family Treatment Center). University of Puerto Rico, Graduate School of Social Work, December 1970.

Lewis, Oscar. *La Vida*. New York: Random House, 1966.

Marin, Rosa C. *Annual Report 1962-1963: Dependent Multi-Problem Families in Puerto Rico*. University of Puerto Rico, Graduate School of Social Work, August 31, 1963.

_____ . *A Family-Centered Treatment Research and Demonstration Project in Puerto Rico with Dependent Multi-Problem Families,* Final Report, 1965-1966. University of Puerto Rico, Graduate School of Social Work, March 31, 1967. Note Appendix A.

_____ . *Familias menesterosas con problemas múltiples* (Needy families with multiple problems). *Humanidad,* December 1968, 2nd year, No. 2.

Seplowin, Virginia Montero. *La Aplicación de la Escala de Predicción Social Glueck a 50 Menores* (The Application of the Glueck Social Prediction Scale to 50 Youngsters). University of Puerto Rico, Graduate School of Social Work, May 1960.

U.S. Bureau of the Census. Census of Population: 1970: *Detailed Characteristics,* Final Report PC(1)-D53, Puerto Rico. Washington, D.C.: Government Printing Office, 1973.

ISSUES AND PROBLEMS AFFECTING HISPANIC YOUTH:
An Analysis and a Blueprint for Action

John Florez

This paper identifies critical problems and issues facing Hispanic youth, assesses efforts to resolve them, and recommends strategies for action to improve social conditions related to these problems and issues. Before discussing such strategies, it is important to analyze the pervasive social and political forces which, this paper contends, influence how national social policy evolves in this subject area and how related programs are implemented. Furthermore, in looking at the problem of juvenile justice and delinquency prevention as they affect Hispanic youth, it will be clear that what is needed is a national policy on families.

Delinquency and Crime—A Major Youth Issue

Hispanic Americans constitute the youngest of all ethnic populations in this country, having a median age of 20.7 years compared with 28.6 years for the general population. Among Hispanics there is also a fairly wide spread of median age figures indicative of different levels and types of services needed: the median age for Cuban Americans is 36.8 years; for Latinos, 25.5 years; for Mexican Americans, 20.3 years; and for Puerto Ricans, 19.6 years. About 44 percent of the Hispanic population are under age 18, compared to 31 percent for the general population. During the next decade Hispanic families will continue to experience serious social, economic, and health problems that have severe impact on our youth and children—higher morbidity and mortality rates, a growing incidence of one-parent families, higher rates of unemployment and underemployment, school dropouts, runaways, and a higher rate of substance abuse, to cite only a few (National Council of Organizations for Children and Youth, 1976). Most alarming and far-reaching of all the problems confronting these families are the projections made with regard to delinquency and crime. Although by 1990 an overall decrease in delinquency is projected, the following factors will be prominent: (1) delinquency and youth crime will increase in the inner cities; (2) both will be on the rise for racial and ethnic minority groups in particular; (3) youth crime will be of a grave nature, i.e., homicide, rape, armed robbery, and serious assault; and (4) victims of such crimes will be largely other young people (Zimmering, 1975).

It is believed that Hispanic youth are more likely to be arrested and detained than their Anglo counterparts. Studies by Ohlin and Miller (1976) suggest that whether or not a youth is detained is based on two factors: (1) the socio-economic background of the youth and (2) the availability of detention facilities. Accordingly, since Hispanic youth are more likely to be poor and to live in urban settings where detention facilities are more available, the likelihood of their being detained is greatly increased. These studies further point out that youth detained in secure facilities are more likely to be subsequently placed in secure settings, e.g., institutions vs. group homes.

Given these facts, it is hoped that elected officials and public administrators will exercise leadership in tackling the serious problem of juvenile delinquency and youth crime. As for the Hispanic community, it is imperative that we recognize this problem as a major issue to be addressed now and in the near future.

Obstacles to Effective Solutions

In any review and assessment of past national efforts to confront juvenile delinquency, it is useful to analyze the evolution of these efforts in order to understand how social and political forces have influenced the outcomes. Efforts at solving this—or any other social problem, for that matter—have been hampered by a combination of forces that may or may not be unique to the American scene:

- Heavy reliance on the ethic of pragmatism and impatience, i.e., if there is a problem, there must be an immediate solution.
- Strong acceptance of specialization or a belief in professionals.
- A vast network of bureaucracies where people are estranged from the governmental process and many lack adequate information on their rights and on available programs and resources.
- Little accountability in government agencies providing social services to the public.

Because these forces tend to prevail in the delivery of human services, there is a breakdown in efforts to rationalize the delivery system in accord with its true intent, i.e., to match the help provided with the genuine needs of individuals and families. In addition, there has developed a vast, inefficient network of "patched-on" programs that have little or no relationship to one another, that frequently work at cross-purposes to one another, and that have spawned an industry of middlemen who profit from and thus help maintain the bureaucratic maze. Finally, and most significantly, these forces have had the effect of weakening the family as the social institution that initially provides for the basic development and maturation of children and youth as adequately functioning social beings. If nothing else, this is a most devastating indictment of the failure of our human services system.

Let us examine these social and political forces which actually determine what directions ameliorative programs will take. This analysis will enable us to develop more practical strategies for action to combat youth problems.

Pragmatism and Impatience

There are no easy solutions to the problems we face as a people. There is an almost overpowering temptation to believe that somewhere along the line we made one big mistake, forgot one big truth, overlooked the one key to salvation. We want a simple answer. Seeking such simplicity, ardent but undisciplined minds seize on every new and fashionable nostrum that floats by (Gardner, 1970).

Efforts now underway to address youth problems are failing not just Hispanic youth, but all youth. Consider the following factors. In any given community, you will find a patchwork of agencies providing all kinds of human services. For nearly every human problem, you will find an agency created to provide a service, be it in the private sector or at the local, county, State, or Federal level. However, the services of these agencies are usually provided only after the person in need has been diagnosed and "labeled," e.g., in the case of young people, this often means marked as a delinquent, dropout, runaway, etc. To continue the example, a delinquent youth will obtain counseling only after being labeled as such; a youth will not receive special education until first classified as a school dropout; or a parent will not receive family-oriented counseling until there is a serious family breakdown, rupture, or even mental illness.

However well-intentioned some of these programs have been, let us look at some of their effects on American family structure. In the early 1960s it was asserted that minority children were culturally deprived. In response, a special focus program was developed—Head Start. Experts then found that children's nutrition problems affected their learning capabilities, and soon another program was created—the school hot lunch program. In each of these instances the underlying attitude was "If there is a problem, there must be an immediate solution." Each of these programs supplanted a function that the family normally exercises. Instead of designing and implementing a comprehensive program that would allow and assist the family to fulfill its vital functions in such areas as education, role model instruction, and the provision of life's daily necessities, experts developed a host of separate programs that resulted in a further debilitation of familial functioning.

It is this kind of simplistic thinking that has made it difficult for many professionals or experts to provide services to Hispanic families. In many cases, they want to examine the culture of these families and come to rapid conclusions. It is assumed that if the cultural elements that determine the structure and functions of Hispanic families are isolated and analyzed, then one would be able to provide services to these families. Unfortunately, this kind of thinking is tantamount to "If you have seen one, you have seen them all" and does not recognize the dynamics of diversity in our Hispanic cultural context.

Specialization and Professionalism

Americans are taught to have an implicit faith and confidence in professionals as well as a keen appreciation for the high degree of specialization required to maintain and expand our technological society. As a result, many tend to believe that only the experts know best and, increasingly, many are content to let the experts make decisions without their involvement or consent. When people fail to benefit from the services provided, usually the consumers are blamed for the failure, not the professionals providing services. In fact, there is little incentive for many professionals to question whether or not their practices should be changed. Too often these professionals have near-monopoly control over the services they provide.

Moreover, because service systems are broken down into specialties, people usually can obtain services only after their problems have been isolated and relegated to this or that category of service need and an approach has been made to the agency specializing in serving a particular category. This has led to the fragmentation of services, agency jurisdictional jealousies, and, more importantly, an emphasis on providing services only after problems have appeared. What is needed is an array of services oriented toward prevention and readily accessible to people in need. The "general practitioner" is needed in the helping services.

Bureaucracies and Accountability

We live in a society that has a vast bureaucracy charged with many responsibilities. When these are not properly discharged, it is the poor and helpless who are more likely to be hurt and who have no remedy . . . .

We need to create new remedies to deal with the multitude of daily injuries that persons suffer in this complex society simply because it is complex.

I am not talking about people who injure others out of selfish or evil motives. I am talking about the injuries which result simply from administrative convenience, injuries which may be done inadvertently by those endeavoring to help—teachers, social workers, and urban planners (Kennedy, 1964).

We must face the reality that bureaucratic systems will always be with us due to the complex nature of our society, but at the same time we must continually ask, "How can we make them sensitive and responsive to people?" John Gardner (1970) has pointed out:

All institutions, religious or commercial, political or educational, are extremely skillful in protecting themselves from the proddings of dissent.

The most impenetrable defense is deafness—not anger, not indignation, not punishment, but just inability to hear. Such functional deafness is familiar to every corporate executive or government official who has tried to force a reexamination of policies.

Another major obstacle to overcome in the delivery of services, especially in relation to Hispanics and other minorities, is the inability of bureaucracies to respond to individual needs and cultural differences. Aside from the familiar "benign neglect," government bureaucracies tend to be more insulated against change because, in essence, they function as monopolies and are more responsive to pressures from the top than from the individuals they serve or assist throughout the country. Public monopolies of this type—for example, social services—are seldom called to account because citizens are usually too far removed for significant impact.

Assessing the National Effort Against Juvenile Delinquency

The U.S. House of Representatives Report 95-313 (1977) provides a brief chronology of highlights of past national activities directed at the juvenile delinquency problem:

1912—Creation of the Children's Bureau.
1948—Establishment of the Interdepartmental Committee on Children and Youth.
1950—Mid-Century White House Conference on Children and Youth.
1961—Passage of Juvenile Delinquency and Youth Offenses Control Act (P.L. 87-274).
1968—Passage of the Juvenile Delinquency Prevention Control Act (P.L. 90-445) which delegated responsibility to the U.S. Department of Health, Education, and Welfare to establish a national juvenile delinquency prevention program.
1968—Passage of the Omnibus Crime Control and Safe Streets Act (P.L. 90-351).
1971—Amendment of the Omnibus Crime Bill to include prevention, control, and reduction of juvenile delinquency; also to include creation of an interdepartmental council to coordinate all Federal juvenile delinquency programs. (Refer to P.L. 91-644).
1973—Amendment of the Omnibus Crime Bill to require States to add juvenile delinquency components to their State plans for the improvement of law enforcement and criminal justice systems. (Refer to P.L. 93-83).
1974—Passage of the Juvenile Justice and Delinquency Prevention Act (P.L. 93-415) and establishment of the Office of the same name within the Law Enforcement Assistance Administration of the U.S. Department of Justice.

Despite the length of time that has elapsed, the national effort in this area has been sporadic, and a proliferation of programs has developed. The first Annual Report of the Office of Juvenile Justice and Delinquency Prevention (1975) dramatically underscores the dilemma in defining the Federal effort: "Federal money spent on or around the juvenile delinquency problem in fiscal year 1975 totals somewhere between $92 million and $20 billion." How could such discrepancy come about? According to the report:

> There are two principal reasons for this huge discrepancy in estimates. The first is that programs to prevent delinquency have a very different focus than programs to respond to delinquency, and this difference interferes with comparisons of program-level budget totals. A million dollars spent on salaries for juvenile probation officers may or may not be more 'useful' in combating delinquency than a million dollars spent on salaries for teachers in ghetto schools. However, the proportions of the money that should be included in a 'delinquency expenditures' category are clearly different.

Another major reason for the discrepancy in estimates is simply that there is no clear-cut definition of the term "juvenile delinquency." This becomes a crucial issue in then attempting to determine how Federal agencies can identify their particular roles in addressing the problem. Dr. Franklin Zimmering (1975) points out the need to re-define what is commonly meant by juvenile delinquency prevention. He suggests that a national effort should focus on "loss reduction" as opposed to juvenile delinquency:

> I consider this an improvement, because it shifts the focus from the young offender to the consequences of his offense. This shift facilitates weighing the total impact of a criminal act against the social price of prevention. It also facilitates development of a greater variety of prevention strategies and competition on an equal footing between non-treatment approaches and treatment programs. Aside from these advantages, the concept of loss reduction is not burdened with the catholicity and non-specificity of 'delinquent prevention.'

In further discussions with Dr. Zimmering, he suggested that what is needed is a "national youth policy." The basic argument is that there are services required by youth, regardless of whether they may be labeled delinquent or whether they have committed a crime. Expanding on this notion, it is this author's contention that what is needed is a *national family policy.* Through such a policy, we could concentrate on familial support and assistance and reduce emphasis and reliance on responding only to symptoms of dysfunctioning and providing services only to persons after they have experienced a social problem. Through such a policy, Federal efforts could be focused on bolstering family life as opposed to past efforts that created programs whose main result has been to usurp family functions. In short, if we are to be effective in helping youth cope with problems on a daily and individual basis and if we are to eliminate the fragmentation of Federal efforts, we must plan to treat the family and its members as a unit.

Strategies for Action

It is increasingly apparent that, first of all, we need an overall national strategy aimed at generating family policy development at the Federal level. This would aid the Government in redirecting its efforts toward strengthening, rather than weakening, families. It also would encourage the Government to focus on providing services to all in need, e.g., the Labor Department could help all youths who needed work to find jobs and provide remedial programs for all youth needing them, not just for delinquent youth or school dropouts.

Although there is consensus on the need for coordination and concentration of government efforts in this area, the lack of same continues and even grows worse. Why? Any national strategy to influence national policy must address this question. Because the directions that programs take are often dictated by factors other than programmatic considerations, this paper has previously examined major social and political forces influencing these directions. Hispanics and other minorities have been excluded from meaningful roles in shaping and channeling these forces in the past; however, we are rapidly gaining sophistication in this arena. We can no longer simply demand that we be given a special program, a pilot program, or a crash program—as long as we pursue this strategy, we are only relying on a pittance which can be cut off at any time. We must begin identifying appropriate alliances, forming coalitions, and obtaining positions where we can play key roles in the political process in which decisions are made on policy and programs.

What are major steps that should be taken by members of the Hispanic community and by public administrators as well in resolving problems and concerns affecting Hispanic youth? I would list the following:

1. Convene a national-level workshop or similar gathering to bring together experts to discuss and develop strategies needed to launch an initiative aimed at establishing a national network of agencies, organizations, and groups working with and for Hispanic youth.

2. Begin formulating components of a national family policy and work for its implementation.

3. Gather data that specifically address problems of Hispanic communities affecting families and youth.

4. Provide leadership in research and demonstration efforts to assist Hispanic youth.

5. Form bodies, such as advisory groups, to provide insights on how to work effectively with Hispanic communities at local, regional, and national levels.

6. Develop better methods for subcontracting for services in order to foster a competitive climate that will result in better products.

7. Fund projects and studies to ascertain why Hispanic youth are more likely to be arrested, more likely to be detained, and more likely to be institutionalized instead of being placed in familial or communal settings.

8. Encourage the Office of Juvenile Justice and Delinquency Prevention to work closely with other Federal agencies with statutory authority and interests in the subject area for the purpose of providing improved orientation and assistance to State juvenile justice advisory board members. This should include training members to identify and coordinate local resources, e.g., CETA funds, community development funds, Title XX funds, etc., on behalf on improving youth services. State advisory board participants receiving such training should involve Hispanic youth.

Although these strategies are broad and ambitious, they need to be undertaken if we are to begin to grapple with the problems and concerns of youth in our communities.

REFERENCES

Gardner, John W. *The Recovery of Confidence.* New York: W.W. Norton and Company, Inc., 1970.

Kennedy, Robert F. Attorney General's address on Law Day, University of Chicago Law School, 1964.

National Council of Organizations for Children and Youth. *America's Children, 1976.* Washington, D.C.: the National Council, 1976.

Ohlin, Lloyd, and Miller, Alden. Background material for strategic issues in deinstitutionalization, the case of Massachusetts. Unpublished paper, 1976.

U.S. Congress, House of Representatives. *Report 95-313.* Washington, D.C.: Government Printing Office, 1977.

U.S. Department of Justice, Law Enforcement Assistance Administration. *First Annual Report of the Office of Juvenile Justice and Delinquency Prevention, September 30, 1975,* Vol. 1. Washington, D.C.: the Department, 1975.

Zimmering, Franklin E. Dealing with youth crime, national needs, and Federal priorities. Unpublished paper submitted to the Coordinating Council on Juvenile Justice and Delinquency Prevention, September 1975.

AGE, HEALTH, AND CULTURE:
An Examination of Health Among Spanish-Speaking Elderly

Fernando Manuel Torres-Gil

This paper examines the health status of Spanish-speaking elderly by focusing on utilization of health care facilities, barriers to utilization, and the need for health services. Given the fact that little has been written on this topic, a review of the general literature on health and Hispanics is presented and specific factors affecting utilization are identified. Data from three surveys are used to illustrate health problems and health-related issues among Mexican American elderly. Various factors (such as lack of income and transportation, folk medicine, culture, the family, and discouraging institutional policies) are identified as playing a role in the ability of elderly persons to use health care facilities. A conceptualization of the health cycle in three distinct phases (prevention, initial utilization, and maintenance) is developed to address the question of which factor affecting utilization is important in any given phase. Coping mechanisms (folk medicine, the family, and the church) are also described as resources that help Hispanic elderly survive a health care system that tends to exclude them. Recommendations on improving access to health care are offered to planners and decision makers in this field.

Overview of the Situation of Hispanic Elderly

There is sufficient evidence to indicate that Chicanos, Puerto Ricans, and other Latinos suffer severe health and mental health problems which are not adequately addressed by health and mental health service delivery systems in the United States. More often than not, these systems are not sensitive to the special cultural, economic, and social pressures facing Spanish-speaking individuals. It is appropriate, therefore, that COSSMHO's National Conference on Health and Human Services has been convened to help lay the basis for the formulation of more effective health, mental health, and human service policies for Hispanics. It is especially admirable that particular attention is given to the Hispanic aged, *las personas de mayor edad.* This group rightly symbolizes our culture and our past while, at the same time, it bears the brunt of many of the problems we Hispanics face today—the breakup of the traditional extended family, forced acculturation, insensitive government practices, citizenship difficulties, lack of adequate housing and transportation, low educational opportunities, and language discrimination.

Author's Note. Special acknowledgment is given to Francisco Nunez, Ph.D. candidate at the University of Southern California, for his invaluable research assistance and to Jose Duarte, Executive Director of the East Los Angeles Health Task Force, for making this study possible.

According to the Bureau of the Census (1973), there were approximately 404,000 Spanish origin persons age 65 and older living in the continental United States in 1970. Of these, about 189,000 were of Mexican origin; slightly more than 34,000, of Puerto Rican origin; and about 35,000, of Cuban origin. This was out of an estimated Spanish origin population of over nine million persons, nearly half of whom were of Mexican origin. Of course, these figures must be viewed cautiously because the use of inadequate census procedures has resulted in a serious undercount of the Spanish origin population. This is especially true of those Hispanics in this country who do not have legal entry documentation. Many older Latinos are reluctant to participate in census studies because of fear of deportation. Nevertheless, existing demographic information about Hispanic elderly reveals a very low socioeconomic level. Thirty-two percent of them are classified as poor, compared to 25 percent of the Anglo elderly population so classified; for Mexican American elderly alone, the figure is much higher—37 percent. Approximately 16 percent of Hispanic men and women age 65 and older have completed high school, compared to 28 percent of the Anglo elderly population; only seven percent of the Mexican American elderly reached this educational level.

Like the elderly everywhere, Spanish-speaking elderly face many problems associated with old age. They are confronted with the increasing difficulties of illness (often chronic) and other physical disabilities. Many live in substandard housing which they cannot afford to repair, particularly in the *barrios* of larger cities. Others are forced to rely on public or subsidized housing for shelter, while still others live with family or relatives. With increasing age comes the loss of reflexes, perception, and skills necessary for driving. Thus, many are forced to rely on public transportation—bus or taxi—which may be either inaccessible or too expensive. Alternately, they may be forced to rely on their extended family for transportation, a situation that may serve to undercut their sense of independence.

As is well known, elderly individuals of all races are often ignored by American society which places such great value on youth, energy, and glamor. Older people, in general, must face many negative stereotypes that contribute to their unfortunate plight. They are often viewed as senile, conservative, asexual, apolitical, and even useless. The respected and valued roles that older people once held in the professions, the family, and society are largely a thing of the past. In this regard, older Latinos have some advantages because they are tied more closely than their white counterparts to traditions and customs that provide a respected and even exalted position for them. In many areas of the country, especially rural areas, one can still find the older person acting as an authority figure, matriarch or patriarch, provider, transmitter of culture, and counselor—all of which are positions that give the individual a valuable role in the community (Sotomayor, 1973). Shelter, food, and love are reciprocated between the older person and the family, between the older person and the *barrio*. But even among the Spanish-speaking, it appears that in some areas (particularly in urban areas of the Southwest and the East Coast) these traditions are breaking down. There is disquieting evidence that the older person is becoming more isolated and alienated than had once been the case. More elderly Latinos find themselves living alone in housing projects or in subsidized housing with little interaction between them and

84

other family members. Urbanization and acculturation of the young combine to lessen the valued roles of older Latinos. In addition, Spanish-speaking elderly must face problems unique to them. Many were born outside the United States and thus have citizenship problems. In particular, Mexican American elderly tend to be wary of immigration authorities who may threaten them with deportation or loss of citizenship.*

Among all the problems facing Hispanic elderly, health is perhaps one of the most troublesome. The normal infirmities brought on by advancing age are compounded by the social and cultural difficulties previously cited. Unfortunately, very little research has been undertaken to explore this pressing area of social concern. Nor is there a quantity of data to help document the nature, type, and frequency of specific problems.   Not surprisingly, given the state of research in this area, there is as yet no comprehensive review of the literature on the health and mental health status of the Spanish-speaking elderly population. The initial review that follows, therefore, will help to point out vast gaps in our knowledge as well as help to establish a background for further examination of the issues.

Literature Review

To date, attention has not been paid to the health and mental health situation of older Spanish-speaking persons as distinct from the Spanish-speaking population as a whole. Issues such as the availability and utilization of services have not been explored. No research to speak of has addressed itself to the problems facing Hispanic elderly groups other than Chicanos.** Instead, the literature has focused almost entirely on the subculture of health among Mexican Americans (folk medicine, fatalism, religion), utilization of mental health facilities, and explanations for the lack of services.

Weaver (1973) provides a useful categorization of research on health care behavior among Mexican Americans. He describes and critiques three generations of research orientation. The first, primarily in the 1940s but continuing into the 1950s, is identified as anthropological in approach with a reliance on cultural attributes to distinguish and explain health care behavior. Saunders (1953, 1954, 1956) placed health care behavior in a cultural perspective and developed a theory that there are four basic sources of Chicano health care knowledge and treatment: (1) folk medicine of Mexico; (2) folk medicine of one or more Native American tribes; (3) Anglo folk medicine; and (4) scientific medicine. In this light, Saunders focused on folk medicine culture and its impact on preventive health. He perceived the more negative aspects of folk culture, such as diseases caused by magic about which little could be done, and the negative aspects of family and time, e.g., illness seen as a social event, thus giving rise to the avoidance of hospitalization and the *mañana* syndrome.

Editor's note. For background on the origins of this fear, see two other papers in this volume: *Hispanic Families: An Exploration* by Ismael Dieppa and Miguel Montiel and *Chicanos in the United States: An Overview of Socio-Historical Context and Emerging Perspectives* by Miguel Montiel.

**Due to the paucity of previous work on health problems of mainland Puerto Rican, Cuban, or other Latino elderly, the remainder of this paper must be limited to the situation of Mexican American elderly. Future uses of the term "Spanish-speaking elderly" thus refer only to this latter group.

The second generation of health studies, conducted in the late 1950s and continuing into the 1960s, is characterized by Clark's study in a San Jose *barrio* (1959), Madsen's in south Texas (1964), and Rubel's in Hidalgo County, Texas (1966). These studies, patterned after Saunders' work and in many cases built on his findings, concentrated on folk medicine and attempted a cultural interpretation of health care behavior. They supported the subculture thesis that patients treat themselves, are treated by family or friends, or visit *curanderos* and that they are not concerned about time or efficiency. All these factors were then seen as forming a barrier to effective utilization of scientific health care. In retrospect, these studies are notable for two reasons: (1) they continued to rely on participant observations of small samples; and (2) they had a large impact on a generation of students and academicians who utilized and overgeneralized their findings, thus contributing to myths and stereotypes about Spanish-speaking persons.

Jaco (1959) was one of the first to rely on survey research rather than on anthropological methodology. Whereas others had relied on small samples of rural working class or peasant Mexican Americans, he utilized approximately 11,000 records of psychotic patients and created a comparable profile of the incidence of mental illness. His main finding was that Mexican Americans had lower rates of commitment to mental institutions, a fact he interpreted as meaning they had lower levels of psychotic disturbances than Anglos. Jaco also relied on a negative view of Mexican culture, symbolized by Rubel's comment that a major task of South Texas Valley physicians should be to change the culture in order to apply scientific health practices effectively.

The third generation of research on Mexican American health needs is characterized by Weaver as the "emergence of the Chicano." He stated that this generation, developing in the 1960s, utilized survey research, contradicted as well as confirmed previous research, and continued to concentrate on narrow segments of the population. In addition, he noted the influence of *Chicanismo* on the orientation and interpretation of this era's research. Survey research by Moustafa and Weiss (1968) investigated mortality and utilization rates. Clark (1959) examined the fear that Mexican Americans exhibited with regard to health workers and investigators. Nall and Speilberg (1967) argued that the family had a negative impact on health care, and Kiev (1968) more elaborately identified fatalism, oedipal patterns, *dignidad,* stoicism, and other cultural traits as having a negative impact on health care practices. On a more positive side, Karno and Edgerton (1969) utilized survey research to examine mental health practices of Mexican Americans and found a marked underutilization of psychiatric facilities. Other recent research has shown a greater concern about the importance of investigating such variables as class, education, age, residence, and family size, as well as an increased awareness of the stereotypes, misinterpretations, and overgeneralizations that plagued prior research.

In research related to mental health, the literature focuses on the relative incidence of psychological services utilization by Mexican Americans. Some found a lower rate (Jaco, 1959; Karno and Edgerton, 1969), while others found a higher rate (Saunders, 1954; Wingnall and Koppin, 1967). A few writers have suggested that the family provides support in the face of mental breakdown (Jaco, 1959, 1960; Madsen, 1964), while others have suggested that faith healers rather than professionals may explain underutilization (Karno and Edgerton, 1969).

This brief review of the literature serves to highlight several issues critical to any discussion of the health status of Mexican American elderly. Most obvious is the fact that none of these published works deal exclusively with older Spanish-speaking persons. A serious lack of knowledge has existed for many years about this group, their health status, needs, and problems. References are seldom made to age as a variable nor are the roles of the elderly in the family, culture, or society discussed. Little has been known about their access to health facilities or their distinctions between health and mental health, both of which are areas of prime importance. Few, if any, studies have made use of medical examinations, medical services utilization, or the relative importance of various factors (such as socio-economic status, age, and language) in health services utilization. Most research has focused on the characteristics of "traditional" Mexican American culture that may affect the interactions of Mexican Americans with the Anglo-oriented health care delivery system. Previous research has also had a disregard for policy-oriented issues: What programs are best suited for such older persons? Where should such programs and services be located? Who will fund such programs and services, given the lack of financial resources in the *barrios?*

Health Status Among Mexican American Elderly

Health care delivery systems in this country are theoretically designed to serve all segments of society—rich and poor, minority and non-minority, the more educated and the less educated. Access to these systems is supposedly open to all. In the real world, however, this is frequently not the case. To a large degree, Chicanos and other minorities are effectively excluded.

The current standard health care delivery system contains many entry and treatment points: clinics, general hospitals, optometry and podiatry clinics, pharmacies, long-term care facilities, specialized medical facilities, and public health facilities, among others. This system, with its myriad services and entry points, becomes complicated and expensive to navigate. Bilingual/bicultural persons appear to be excluded from these services because of the system's complicated and costly nature as well as its insensitivity to many social, cultural, and political features unique to Spanish-speaking elderly.

The data presented here are derived from surveys taken in three geographical areas—Colorado; San Antonio, Texas; and East/Northeast Los Angeles, California. The Colorado study (Interstate Research Associates, 1974) took the form of personal interviews conducted in late 1973 and early 1974. The total sample included 1,420 persons age 55 and older—65 percent of whom were Mexican Americans; 20 percent, Asians; and 15 percent, Native Americans. The San Antonio study (Gomez, Martin, and Gibson, 1973) featured interviews with 200 Chicanos age 55 and older (123 women and 77 men). The East Los Angeles Health Task Force study (1975), which provides the majority of the data presented here, utilized a representative stratified sample of 179 Mexican Americans age 44 and older.

How did Mexican American elderly respondents in these studies perceive their health status? In San Antonio, 35 percent of the women and

46 percent of the men categorized their health as poor. In East Los Angeles, 37.5 percent of the men over age 60 and 46 percent of the women categorized their health as poor to very poor; in addition; 53 percent of the men and 41 percent of the women considered themselves disabled. When asked if a health provider, at any time within the last year, had judged them as being disabled, these elderly answered affirmatively in almost the same proportions as when asked if they considered themselves disabled.

What were some of the major health-related physical problems cited? The Colorado study showed that difficulty getting up and down stairs was the most frequently mentioned (31.5 percent), followed by shopping for groceries (28.9 percent), vision (27.8 percent), hearing (24.2 percent), eating solid foods (21.2 percent), remembering (19.8 percent), and getting out of the house (19.8 percent). The mean number of difficulties per person was 2.1 with no sex differences. In East Los Angeles, among 64 respondents who considered themselves disabled (including the total sample of persons aged 45-59 and 60+), the major problems were arthritis and related diseases (18 percent), followed by diabetes mellitus (11 percent), cardiovascular diseases (11 percent), nervousness and debility (9 percent), accidents and injuries (6 percent), and cerebrovascular diseases (5 percent).

The data from these studies show rather conclusively that the health situation of the older Mexican American—whether in rural areas of Colorado or in urban areas of Texas and California—is far from good. Such findings are not altogether surprising, given the age and low socio-economic status of this group. But these data barely scratch the surface. Other issues related to the availability and utilization of health care services must be explored further. More specifically, we need to look more closely at such issues as: the desire of the Chicano population for more effective health care in both treatment and prevention; barriers to utilization of health care facilities; the failure of researchers, planners, and decision makers to improve accessibility to the health care delivery system; and reliance by older Mexican Americans on available coping mechanisms (the family, folk medicine, and religion).

Utilization of Health Services

To what extent do older Mexican Americans use health services? The 1975 East Los Angeles Health Task Force (ELAHTF) study provides some answers.

As Table I indicates, physicians and optometrists were the health professionals consulted most frequently. The mean number of consultations for Chicano males age 60 and older was 13; for females, 8. Of note in the table is the wide use of physicians—a finding consistent with findings of a larger study of Los Angeles County households showing consultation of physicians to be the most frequent form of health services used by older people (County of Los Angeles Department of Health Services, 1976). Some observers have suggested that physicians are perceived by elderly Mexican Americans as a "cure-all" or a centralized health resource for all illness not treatable in the home, including mental health problems. The data tend to confirm such impressions.

When asked their reasons for consulting a physician within the last year, the men age 60 and older responded: diabetes (7), gastro-intestinal diseases (6), musculo-skeletal arthritis (5), and hypertension (4). The

TABLE I

FREQUENCY OF RESPONSES TO THE QUESTION
"HAVE YOU CONSULTED A _____ WITHIN THE LAST YEAR?"
AMONG CHICANOS AGE 60 AND OLDER IN EAST LOS ANGELES

Sex / Providers	Male (N=32)		Female (N=54)	
	Yes	No	Yes	No
Physician	28 (87.5%)	4 (12.5%)	52 (96.0%)	2 (4.0%)
Dentist	9 (28.0%)	23 (71.8%)	15 (27.8%)	39 (72.2%)
Optometrist	18 (56.2%)	14 (43.7%)	28 (51.9%)	26 (48.1%)

SOURCE: Data from the East Los Angeles Health Task Force study, 1975.

women age 60 and older responded: hypertension (19), general examinations (19), diabetes (14), and influenza/colds (10).

Table II lends further support to the observation that physician consultations are among the most widely used health service among elderly Mexican Americans. Clinics visited included both private and government-controlled facilities, such as county health services or outpatient clinics of public hospitals. Only one person from the total East Los Angeles sample of persons aged 45-59 and 60+ indicated visiting a neighborhood free clinic.

It is interesting to note that approximately 50 percent of the respondents said they received home health care provided by a relative or friend. The relatively high use of this resource may be attributed to the cost of other care, alienation from or lack of access to various forms of institutional care, or the positive supportive role of family and friends. This percentage is significant when compared to the finding that only one male in the 45-59 age group and one male in the 60+ group had been in an extended care facility within the last year. Is this discrepancy in the care of chronic illness among elderly Chicanos brought about because they naturally look to their family members for care? Or does it occur because extended care facilities and nursing homes, although needed, are alienating to them?

The need for health care and the demand and necessity for personal health services are apparent. The large percentage of respondents who perceived their health as poor to very poor, their reliance on physicians, and the prevalence of chronic illnesses which usually require follow-up care—all these factors offer substantial proof of serious health problems. But how readily do Mexican American elderly receive the medical services necessary for the improvement and maintenance of health? The ELAHTF study addressed this issue by asking respondents whether they felt the need for medical services in the past year but did not seek care. Table III indicates the response breakdown for the total sample.

TABLE II

TYPE, SOURCE, AND FREQUENCY OF HEALTH SERVICES RECEIVED AMONG CHICANOS AGE 60 AND OLDER IN EAST LOS ANGELES

Sex / Services Received	Male (N=32)		Female (N=54)	
	Yes	No	Yes	No
Stayed overnight in hospital as patient within last year	13 (40.6%)	19 (59.4%)	11 (20.4%)	43 (79.7%)
Received health care at a clinic within last year	11 (34.3%)	21 (65.6%)	18 (33.3%)	35 (64.8%)
Friend or family member provided home health care while ill within last year	16 (50.0%)	16 (50.0%)	25 (46.3%)	29 (53.6%)

SOURCE: Data from the East Los Angeles Health Task Force study, 1975.

TABLE III

FREQUENCY OF FELT NEED FOR MEDICAL CARE AMONG CHICANOS AGES 45-59 AND 60+ IN EAST LOS ANGELES

Sex / Age	Male (N=74)		Female (N=105)	
	Yes	No	Yes	No
45-59	11 (26%)	31 (74%)	27 (53%)	24 (47%)
60+	10 (31%)	22 (69%)	23 (43%)	31 (57%)

SOURCE: Data from the East Los Angeles Health Task Force study, 1975.

These data dramatically illustrate the felt need for greater health services. Thirty-one percent of the men in the 60+ age group and 43 percent of the women in the same age group felt they did not receive medical care when needed. In the younger age group, where maintenance of health is critical in minimizing the debilitating effects of advancing age, 26 percent of the men and 53 percent of the women felt they did not receive care when needed. In particular, female respondents in both age groups sampled appeared to have the greater felt need for medical attention.

Barriers to Utilization

What factors may account for these perceptions by Mexican American elderly that they are not obtaining needed health care? Is it due to a reliance on folk medicine or the extended family? Are health services delivery planning and implementation insensitive to the needs of this group? Or are services simply inaccessible? Although the ELAHTF study is the only one to document the desire for medical services, it may be generalized that this need is as acute in other locations where large concentrations of Mexican American and other Hispanic elderly reside. It should be remembered that Los Angeles Chicanos reside in an urban environment where economic and social opportunities are supposedly more readily available (Grebler, Moore, and Guzman, 1970) than in other areas of the Southwest. If health care systems are to improve their planning and delivery of services to Spanish-speaking elderly, the factors that affect services utilization must be clearly identified and their relative importance under varying circumstances must be ascertained.

Padilla, Ruiz, and Alvarez (1975), in perhaps the best work on the subject, discussed factors associated with the delivery of mental health services to the Spanish-speaking population. Although their paper focuses on mental health, it proves useful in a more general discussion of utilization of health services among older Mexican Americans. Padilla *et al.* asserted that the Spanish-speaking population received mental health care of a different kind, of lower quality, and in lesser proportions than any other ethnically identifiable population. They identified specific variables which have positive explanations for this underutilization.

Frequency and severity of mental illness. Several reports (Jaco, 1959; Madsen, 1964) found an underutilization of mental health resources and suggest that Mexican Americans are better prepared to tolerate stress and thus require less support from social institutions. Other writers (Karno and Edgerton, 1969) suggest that the Mexican American population is subjected to more stress and tension because of social, economic, and cultural pressures arising from living within a larger white society.

Use of folk medicine and/or faith healers. Reliance on traditional folk culture has been a favorite area of study for many researchers. One result of this emphasis, however, has been the creation of the stereotypic conception that folk remedies are regularly selected as alternative solutions for emotional problems or as substitutes for utilization of the health care system. The role of the family in health behavior, although not included in the study by Padilla *et al.,* can be also considered a cultural factor affecting health practices. The family, especially in earlier studies of health among Mexican Americans, has been considered a source of emotional support which, through its dependency ties, discourages members from utilizing hospitals, psychiatrists, or doctors.

Discouraging institutional policies. This category concerns organizational factors and institutional policies that discourage greater utilization. Long waiting periods, inflexible intake procedures, and the insensitivity of health professionals are examples of such institutional barriers. Factors in this category include:

a. *Geographic isolation.* Health and mental health programs are frequently inaccessible because of their location outside the *barrio*, inadequate transportation services to insure access, or the absence of child care centers.

b. *Language barriers.* Many Mexican American elderly speak Spanish as their first language and speak little or no English. The absence of interpreters or bilingual personnel would directly affect utilization for those with limited or no English-speaking ability.

c. *Class-bound values.* The middle class values of professional staff are seen as conflicting with values associated with persons from a low socioeconomic background. One example frequently mentioned is the formal time schedule followed by hospital and clinical staff which conflicts with the more flexible time schedules which many poor people must follow.

Sudnow (1967), in an article on a county hospital's method of dealing with emergency cases, documented the class bias of medical staff. He concluded that there is a strong relationship between age, social background, the perceived moral character of patients, and the amount of effort expended in emergency care. The elderly and alcoholics were the two groups given the least consideration by the staff. The second-rate care offered in some emergency cases may even have been responsible for some unnecessary patient deaths.

d. *Culture-bound values.* Cultural conflict is seen as occurring when therapists and other professional staff view Spanish-speaking clients as hostile, suspicious, illiterate, and provincial. These conflicts are rooted in the insensitivity of many Anglo professionals to the bilingual/bicultural characteristics of Mexican Americans.

In assessing obstacles to utilization of mental health centers, Padilla *et al.* believe that the alleged ability of Mexican Americans to cope with emotional problems and utilize folk medicine as substitutes for modern medicine are not valid explanations. Instead, they conclude that the major explanatory variables are associated with discouraging institutional policies. In particular, they cite language, class, and culture biases as major factors actively discouraging utilization of mental health services among Mexican Americans.

Although the article previously described focuses on the mental health of the general Chicano population, it provides a framework for identifying specific factors which negatively affect utilization of the health care delivery system by older Mexican Americans. All the factors mentioned are important ingredients in the health care behavior of Mexican American elderly. It is reasonable to assume that the older person is affected by each of the factors described, but in different ways and to different degrees. While data with which to evaluate barriers to the utilization of health services by older Mexican Americans are difficult to obtain, a start in this direction has been made by the previously cited studies in Colorado, Texas, and, in particular, in the East Los Angeles area.

Data from the East Los Angeles Study

In the ELAHTF study a large percentage of Mexican American elderly stated that they did not seek medical care even if they felt a need for it. Their reasons were as follows:

TABLE IV

**REASONS FOR NOT SEEKING MEDICAL CARE
CITED BY CHICANOS AGE 60 AND OLDER IN EAST LOS ANGELES**

Reasons Sex	Male (N=14)	Female (N=33)
Lack of finances and/or insurance	9 (64%)	17 (52%)
Medicare/Medicaid problems	1 (7%)	6 (18%)
Lack of transportation and/or personal assistance	3 (21%)	6 (18%)
Lack of trust with health providers	0 (0%)	2 (6%)
Other	1 (7%)	2 (6%)

SOURCE: Data from the East Los Angeles Health Task Force study, 1975.

As Table IV indicates, the major reason given for not seeking medical services was a lack of finances and/or insurance to pay the costs. The second major reason was the lack of transportation and/or personal assistance.

Another question further probed obstacles to the utilization of health services. Respondents were asked: "In thinking back over your experiences with health providers, what have been the most serious obstacles encountered in obtaining medical care?" The responses are illustrated in the following table.

TABLE V

BARRIERS CITED AS OBSTACLES TO UTILIZATION OF HEALTH SERVICES BY CHICANOS AGE 60 AND OLDER IN EAST LOS ANGELES

Barriers / Sex	Male (N=41)	Female (N=74)
Lack of finances and/or insurance	10 (24%)	23 (31%)
Language barriers	5 (12%)	9 (12%)
Rejected for care/ waiting too long	5 (12%)	6 (8%)
Lack of transportation and/or personal assistance	8 (20%)	13 (18%)
Lack of trust with service provider	5 (12%)	4 (5%)
Medicare/Medicaid problems	4 (10%)	9 (12%)
Insensitivity of person to culture and needs	2 (5%)	3 (7%)
Inadequate care given by provider	2 (5%)	7 (9%)

SOURCE: Data from the East Los Angeles Health Task Force study, 1975.
NOTE: Female respondents reported more than one obstacle.

Again, the most serious obstacles encountered by this sample of Mexican American elderly were (1) the lack of finances and/or insurance with which to pay for the medical services and (2) the lack of transportation and/or personal assistance. Language barriers were another serious obstacle. Lack of income and transportation are correlated with the low socio-economic status of older persons and their need for assistance in walking, driving, taking a bus, or using a taxi. For example, in the Colorado survey the median income for minority aged was $174 per month. In the San Antonio study the mean monthly income for women was $191; for men, $211. In the ELAHTF survey, men 60 years of age and older had a mean yearly family income of $5,983 ($481 monthly); women

94

60 years of age and older had a mean yearly family income of $2,073 ($247 monthly). Clearly, older Mexican Americans in these areas have very low incomes, a factor which affects their ability to pay for these services *and* transportation, assuming they do not have adequate health insurance.

Medicare and Medicaid are intended to provide insurance coverage for hospitalization and medical treatment. However, there is evidence that these programs are only partially assiting older Spanish-speaking persons. The ELAHTF study dramatizes the inadequacy of current health insurance coverage. Twenty-five percent of men age 60 and older and 37 percent of women age 60 and older were not covered by Medicare and/or Medicaid. Ninety-one percent of the men 60+ and 85 percent of the women 60+ had no health insurance other than Medicare or Medicaid. Among the total sample of persons between 45-59 years of age and 60 years and over, 25 percent had no insurance coverage to meet any type of medical expenses, meaning that these had to be paid entirely out-of-pocket.

Clearly, folk medicine and cultural values are not the only important obstacles to health care delivery. In fact, the evidence lends substantial support to the thesis that the inaccessibility of the health care delivery system is primarily responsible for the underutilization phenomenon, rather than the older Mexican American's unwillingness or an inherent inhibitory factor in Mexican American culture.

Coping Mechanisms

The older Mexican American, finding little help from existing health services, has developed a rather intricate set of social mechanisms in order to cope with the onset of age-related health problems. These coping mechanisms are invaluable assets and resources if recognized and incorporated not only into the health care delivery system but also into all social service delivery systems. In the broadest sense, the mechanisms are based on a reliance on family, religion, and culture. Unfortunately, as will be documented, these mechanisms are in danger of dissipating and disappearing, once this age cohort of older persons has passed away. The question arises, therefore, whether today's young and middle-aged Chicanos will continue to use the old coping mechanisms or adopt new ones as they grow older. If the latter becomes true, then most certainly they will have to adjust to Anglo-oriented coping mechanisms that rely on a more impersonal, more profit-oriented relationship, one that is founded more on the governmental bureaucracy than on the individual's family or culture. If the former becomes true, then they must find ways to maintain these more traditional mechanisms or at least adapt them to a changing modern society. It should be stressed that these traditional coping mechanisms should not be seen as a substitute for a more humane, efficient, and expanded health care delivery system. Such a system is vitally needed and must remain our first priority. However, more subjective coping mechanisms need to be recognized, incorporated, and maintained whenever possible.

Folk Medicine and Curanderos

In previous research, especially in the 1950s and the 1960s, folk medicine and *curanderos* were seen as the answer to understanding health care practices among the Spanish-speaking. Unfortunately, the interpretations resulting from such studies created stereotypes and overgeneralizations about the impact of folk medicine on the general Chicano population. However, if examined in a different context—a context which includes folk medicine as one coping mechanism of older persons—we begin to see these cultural manifestations as health resources rather than as novelty items to be studied by anthropologists.

In assessing the health status of older Mexican Americans, the ELAHTF survey attempted to determine the respondents' first choice of action upon developing a health problem. The largest percentage of men (39 percent) and women (50 percent) over 60 years of age answered that they consult a doctor. A surprising percentage (22 percent of the men and 43 percent of the women) also answered that they take teas, *yerbas,* and other home remedies. In the San Antonio study, 80 percent of the women and 70 percent of the men had knowledge of medicinal herbs, their usage, folk illnesses and their cures, and where herbs and treatment could be obtained. These data lead us to conclude that many older persons do indeed believe in folk medicine and utilize its treatments. Illnesses such as *mal de ojo, empache, susto,* and *aire* are treated by oral administration of various herbs: *yerba buena, manzanilla,* and other herbs. Application of liniments, oils, and herbal mixtures, as well as massages *(sobadas)* and diet regulation are also used as treatments. Treatments may be administered by anyone who has the knowledge. A patient may treat himself, ask a friend or relative who knows herbs and other cures, or go to a *curandero* (a specialist in the diagnosis and treatment of folk syndromes). Although the full extent of the use of folk medicine among older Mexican Americans is not known, belief in it has been long-standing and has strong emotional significance.

The Family

As has been the case with folk medicine, the family has often been viewed in the literature as a deterrent to individual adjustment and social mobility among Mexican Americans. The negative or conservative effects of the family have also been used to explain the health attitudes and behavior of Chicanos. Nall and Speilberg (1967), for example, suggested that the presence of relatives in the neighborhood and the process of seeking advice from them on private matters were related to the refusal of hospitalization for treatment of tuberculosis. Murillo (1971) speculated that Chicanos were late for appointments because their concept of responsibility placed primary importance on attending to the immediate needs of their families. To the extent that these findings have validity, they are most applicable to the elderly, since it is this segment of the Mexican American population that has the closest family ties.

However, at the same time, the family clearly plays a very positive role in health care as an invaluable asset in providing financial, emotional, and health care support. The family often is the center of the older person's social world, and, in turn, the older person provides important functions. Sotomayor (1973), in a study of Chicano grandparents in a Denver *barrio,* found that grandparents help in rearing grandchildren, solving family crises, teaching religion, and transmitting cultural heritage (language, values, food customs, history, etc.) The family will often accompany the older person to stores and to welfare offices, the Department of Motor Vehicles, and a variety of economic and social agencies, particularly if the older person does not speak English. In the ELAHTF study, for example, it was found that the family frequently accompanied the older person to a health facility. The study showed that 44 percent of the men and 52 percent of the women age 60 and older did not usually go alone to receive medical care.

There is evidence that researchers are beginning to recognize the family as an important coping mechanism in the utilization of health services. Hoppe and Heller (1975), in a study examining the influences of the family and occupational stability on alienation and health care utilization, found that the family is an important coping mechanism which reduces feelings of alienation among lower-income Mexican Americans and, in turn, influences the health care utilization behavior of this group.

It is hoped that all efforts will be made to encourage the family to assist and participate with the older person in health care maintenance and preventive aspects of health, such as health education. In turn, the breakdown of the extended family in certain areas may be minimized and perhaps averted if government policy avoids regulations which force family members to let the older person handle an agency or institution on his or her own.

The Church

Many, if not most, older Mexican Americans have relatively strong religious beliefs and attend church more often than other segments of the Chicano population (Grebler, Moore, and Guzman, 1970). The church provides as an important spiritual support for many older persons, helping them to face pain, suffering, and emotional crises. In addition to continuing this spiritual support, the church could also act as an important advocate and disseminator of health information because it often has direct access to many older Spanish-speaking persons who could not otherwise be reached (e.g., those without proper immigration or citizenship papers). Education about balanced inexpensive meals, metabolic system needs (exercise and the dangers of obesity), and the location of social and other service agencies are all examples of the consumer education needed in this area—information that the church could help disseminate.

The Health Cycle of Older Persons:
A Conceptualization Approach to Utilization Obstacles

Utilizing data from the ELAHTF and similar surveys provides an invaluable opportunity for identifying barriers in accessing health care delivery systems. However, it is also important to take a broader perspective of the total health cycle of older Mexican Americans. The previously mentioned data reflect only one phase of health care practice. In reality, there are a number of distinct phases in the health cycle of the elderly Mexican American, each affected differently by the previously discussed variables (folk medicine, culture, the family, religion, and institutional policies).

Most data presented in this paper deal with initial utilization of a health facility. A person feels ill or gets hurt and seeks the services of a physician, or goes to a county hospital or a clinic. But this is only one phase of the health cycle, particularly among older persons with a distinct ethnic background. Decision makers, researchers, and planners must recognize that these distinct phases exist and that each requires the examination of a different set of variables in establishing areas for improvement of health care delivery systems.

The Preventive Phase

This phase deals with the prevention of sickness and accidents or at least their minimization. Older persons, because of a decline in physical capacities, are more susceptible to cardiovascular diseases, arthritis, hypertension, and accidents. A number of factors have a key role in adequate prevention: nutrition, housing, income, knowledge of potential medical treatments, familial support, and knowledge of existing health systems.

It has often been suggested that current health care delivery systems are not geared to a high level of involvement in the preventive phase. It seems reasonable to assume, however, that their role in this phase could be significantly augmented by incorporating and utilizing existing coping mechanisms derived from folk medicine, the family, and religion.

The Initial Utilization Phase

This phase has been the focus of the data presented in this paper. It deals with the initial utilization of hospitals, clinics, and physicians. Lack of income, poor transportation, and inadequate health insurance have been shown to be the most important variables affecting initial access to health care.

The Health Maintenance Phase

Health care delivery involves more than treatment of illness. It also involves efforts to minimize the need for treatment of diseases or accidents through positive and pro-active programs of health maintenance. After the initial utilization of the health service, it is critical to the older person that comprehensive follow-up procedures be undertaken and that the patient feels comfortable in whatever health facility he or she may be situated. It is in this phase where culture and class-bound values, as well as language and familial support, play an important role. For example, the attitudes and values of health professionals will have a marked influence in determining the utilization by elderly Chicanos of both outpatient and extended care facilities. Hostility toward Chicanos, insensitivity to cultural and class values, lack of bilingual/bicultural personnel, and discouragement of extended visits by family members will serve to discourage the older person from adequate follow-up care. Padilla et al. (1975) cite frustration among personnel in mental health clinics when faced with high numbers of Spanish-speaking people who fail to return to the facility after an initial visit. The authors blame this situation on the difference in social class characteristics between the mental health professionals and their patients, and on the lack of bilingual/bicultural personnel.

In summary, this conceptualization of three distinct phases in the health cycle of an older person is intended to identify factors that inhibit services utilization and specify the degree of importance given to these factors in each phase. The inability of past research and planning to recognize or accept phases such as these and the way in which varying social and cultural factors influence these phases has prevented a more realistic critique of the health care delivery system, as well as subsequent necessary improvements. It is hoped that planners and researchers will examine these areas further.

Recommendations

Given the current state of knowledge, what policy recommendations can be made for improving access to the health care delivery system on behalf of older Spanish-speaking persons? While highly specific recommendations are perhaps premature, one thing is clear: the health status of Spanish-speaking elderly overlaps with nutrition, income, transportation, culture, and other such variables.

A recent article in the *American Psychologist* (1976) described the American health system as a large, complex set of facilities and services. It is a system often characterized by a lack of internal coordination. For example, in East and Northeast Los Angeles, where the ELAHTF study was conducted, there are 12 hospitals, 14 emergency care facilities, 26 clinics, 17 nursing homes, and three mental health facilities for a population of 361,573 persons, of whom 257,968 (71 percent) are Spanish-speaking. Twenty-one percent are 45 years of age and older; of this figure, 32 percent are 65 years of age and older. The most conspicuous health facility in this area is the mammoth Los Angeles County/University of Southern California (LAC/USC) Medical Center which includes the county general hospital.

Is it any wonder that, on top of all other factors impinging on utilization, an older person speaking little English would find it difficult to know how to use this complex health system? If an elderly Mexican American is in need of health care, must choose a specific facility without knowledge of this vast apparatus, has little money, and finds it difficult to get around, more likely than not he or she will do nothing about the problem, rely on family or friends, or go to the only medical resource with which he or she is familiar, the physician.

It is the writer's contention that lack of coordination of health services and the lack of public knowledge about them serve to discourage older persons from making use of existing facilities. Although there are clinics, mental health centers, and hospitals in East Los Angeles, for example, what is needed is a comprehensive health center which is located near the clientele and offers a variety of services. This center could conceivably include a health component, nutrition center, day care facility, and a mental health clinic, all linked with the community by transportation programs such as Dial-A-Ride.

Mental health needs among older persons highlight the necessity for such a community health vehicle. Observations show that many Latino elderly fail to make a distinction between health and mental health. Moreover, there is still a social stigma attached to mental illness and psychiatrists. Various writers point to the underutilization of mental health services (Jaco, 1959, 1960; Madsen, 1964; Karno and Edgerton, 1969; Padilla *et al.*, 1975). Various explanations have been offered, such as a lack of mental disorders, the use of folk medicine as a substitute, the insensitivity of mental health staff, among others. But for older Mexican Americans, no such examination of utilization has been offered. It is not difficult to imagine, however, that the elderly Chicano's tendency to use physicians for all manners of illness masks a significant underutilization of mental health services. Whether this section of the population evidences a lower frequency of emotional or mental crises seems doubtful. The effects of urbanization and the decline of the extended family almost certainly lead to depression and alienation for many. We can assume with some certainty that a significant portion of elderly Chicanos require mental health services provided by professionals who are sensitive to bilingual/bicultural characteristics and that, therefore, the integration of a mental health component into a comprehensive health system would be an important element in making the system more effective.

Incorporation of nutrition centers would be another important component of such a system because adequate nutrition is vital to prevention of illness and to health maintenance. Nutrition centers also serve to draw out the isolated elderly who seek social companionship. It has been observed that many older persons using nutrition centers and other social service agencies frequently have grandchildren with them. A day care facility would probably encourage utilization by older persons who are babysitting or who frequently care for young children. Although at present it appears that Mexican Americans rarely use extended care facilities or nursing homes, it is likely that this will change in the future. Developing such a facility within or near a comprehensive community health center would serve to keep the elderly close to their resources, neighborhood, and family.

Existing transportation systems such as Dial-A-Ride, jitney services, and subsidized taxi services would be better able to transport elderly people to needed services in a centralized facility. Conversely, the center would be in a position to utilize government funds to establish demand-response transportation programs.

Regardless of the way in which health care delivery systems reorganize to insure greater access by the Spanish-speaking elderly, it is important that certain vital health concerns be taken into account. Ortiz de Hill (1975) lists program and services that are of immediate importance.

- Screening and resources
  - Creation of programs that integrate community resources
  - Development of comprehensive service and treatment plans
  - Identification of personnel needs
  - Establishment of information and education systems as well as the fostering of community awareness of needs of the elderly
- Nutrition
  - Location of congregate meal sites in *barrio* settings
  - Expanded provisions for home-delivered meals
  - Provision of assistance with shopping
  - Consumer education about balanced meals
- Home health care
  - Availability of visiting nurse services
  - Increased utilization of home health aides
  - Telephone reassurance services
- Long-term facilities
  - Opportunities for participation in milieu treatment therapy
  - Development and deployment of activity and community care teams

Also recommended are the following actions:

1. The development of comprehensive care facilities that are close to the *barrio* or in areas with high concentrations of older persons.

2. Coordinated leadership on the part of health systems agencies and area agencies on aging in advocating and planning for such care facilities.

3. The development of demand-response systems of transportation to meet the mobility needs of the elderly, and the coordination of such systems to get them to needed health facilities and services.

4. The development and implementation of preventive measures, such as bilingual educational and information programs, early detection programs, and annual health screening examinations.

5. The increased hiring of personnel who are sensitive to the culture, language, and special needs of Hispanic elderly in health programs that serve them.

6. The enactment of national health insurance to assure universal, comprehensive coverage.

7. Greater consideration by health planners and decision makers of the unique cultural aspects affecting Spanish-speaking elderly, in particular, recognizing and strengthening their varied coping mechanisms.

REFERENCES

American Psychological Association, Task Force on Health Research. Contributions of psychology to health research: patterns, problems, and potentials. *American Psychologist,* 1976, April, 263-74.

Clark, Margaret. *Health in the Mexican American Culture.* Berkeley and Los Angeles: University of California Press, 1959.

County of Los Angeles Department of Health Services. Public knowledge of mental health resources: a survey of Los Angeles County residents. *Evaluation and Research Papers,* 1976, IV, 1(February).

East Los Angeles Health Task Force. *Feasibility Study to Assess the Health Needs of the Spanish-Speaking Elderly in an Urban Setting.* The Community Health Foundation, 3945 Whittier Boulevard, Los Angeles, California 90023.

Gomez, Ernesto; Martin, Harry; and Gibson, Guadalupe. Adaption of older Mexican Americans: some implications for social and health programs. San Antonio, Texas: El Centro del Barrio, 1973. (Unpublished manuscript.)

Grebler, Leo; Moore, Joan W.; and Guzman, Ralph C. *The Mexican American People: The Nation's Second Largest Minority.* New York: Free Press, 1970.

Hoppe, Sue K., and Heller, Peter L. Alienation, familism, and the utilization of health services by Mexican Americans. *Journal of Health and Social Behavior,* 1975, *16*(3), 304-314.

Interstate Research Associates. Summary of the 1974 Colorado state survey of minority elderly. Report by IRA, Denver, Colorado, 1974.

Jaco, E. Gartly. Mental health of the Spanish Americans in Texas. *In* Marvin K. Opler (ed.), *Culture and Mental Health: Cross-Cultural Studies.* New York: Macmillan Company, 1959.

_____ . *The Social Epidemiology of Mental Disorder: A Psychiatric Survey of Texas.* New York: Russell Sage Foundation, 1960.

Karno, Marvin and Edgerton, R.B. Perception of mental illness in a

Mexican American community. *Archives of General Psychiatry,* 1969, *20*(2), 233-38.

Kiev, Ari. *Curanderismo: Mexican American Folk Psychiatry.* New York: Free Press, 1968.

Madsen, William. *Mexican Americans of South Texas.* New York: Holt, Rinehart, and Winston, 1964.

Moustafa, A., and Weiss, Gertrude. *Health Status and Practices of Mexican Americans,* Advance Report, Vol. II. Los Angeles: University of California, School of Public Health, February 1968.

Murillo, Nathan. The Mexican American family. *In* Nathaniel Wagner and Marcha Haug (eds.), *Chicanos: Social and Psychological Perspectives.* St. Louis, Missouri: C.V. Mosby and Company, 1971.

Ortiz de Hill, Adelina. Vital health concerns. *In* John Mendoza, William Gomez, and Ascencion Hernandez (eds.), *Proceedings of the National Conference on the Spanish-Speaking Elderly.* Shawnee Mission, Kansas: National Chicano Social Planning Council, 1975.

Nall, Frank C., and Speilberg, Joseph. Social and cultural factors in the responses of Mexican Americans to medical treatment. *Journal of Health and Human Behavior,* 1967, *8*(4), 299-308.

Padilla, A.M.; Ruiz, R.A.; and Alvarez, R. Community mental health services for the Spanish-speaking/surnamed population. *American Psychologist,* 1975, *30*(9), 892-905.

Rubel, Arthur J. *Across the Track: Mexican Americans in a Texas City.* Austin: University of Texas Press, 1966.

Saunders, Lyle. *Cultural Differences and Medical Care: The Case of the Spanish-Speaking People of the Southwest.* New York: Russell Sage Foundation, 1954.

Saunders, Lyle and Hewes, G. Folk medicine and medical practices. *Journal of Medical Education,* 1953, *28* (September), 43-46.

Saunders, Lyle and Samora, Julian. A medical care program for a Colorado county. *In* Benjamin D. Paul (ed.), *Health, Culture, and Community: Case Studies of Public Reaction to Health Programs.* New York: Russell Sage Foundation, 1956.

Sotomayor, Marta. A study of Chicano grandparents in a urban barrio. Unpublished doctoral dissertation, University of Denver, Colorado, August 1973. Available through University Microfilms, Ann Arbor, Michigan.

Sudnow, David. Dead on arrival. *Trans-Action,* 1967, *4,* 11 (November), 6-18.

U.S. Bureau of the Census. Census of Population: 1970, *Subject Reports,* Final Report PC(2)-1C, "Persons of Spanish Origin." Washington, D.C.: Government Printing Office, 1973.

Weaver, Jerry. Mexican American health care behavior: a critical review of the literature. *Social Science Quarterly,* 1973, *54,* 1(June), 84-102.

Wingnall, C.M., and Koppin, L.L. Mexican American usage of state mental hospital facilities. *Community Mental Health Journal,* 1967, *3*(2), 137-48.

ESTABLISHING A BASIS FOR ASSESSING THE RESPONSIVENESS OF OLDER AMERICANS ACT PROGRAMS TO HISPANIC AND OTHER MINORITY ELDERLY

George Thomas Beall

Between 1900 and 1970, as the total population of the United States nearly tripled in size, the older part of the population (persons age 65 and older) grew to almost seven times its size in 1900 (Brotman, 1975). As the population of older persons continues to grow in both absolute and relative numbers, the problems associated with an increasingly aged population are multiplying many times over. Assuring adequate income in retirement, appropriate health care, suitable housing and other forms of living accommodations, effective and efficient social services, including accessible transportation—these and other needs of older persons are recognized as mounting national problems. For those elderly who are also members of racial and ethnic minority groups, the problems of aging are intensified. Because minority elderly are exposed to a form of multiple jeopardy due to age, race, ethnic origin, language, and widespread stereotyping, the barriers to be overcome in responding to their needs are compounded.

Spanish-heritage elderly have been identified as a particularly vulnerable group of older persons. Due to linguistic and cultural barriers, geographic location, and the handicaps endemic to minority group status in this country, they have been described as being in even more deplorable circumstances than are the majority of the elderly population. Most importantly, they have been characterized as unable to relate to the "system"; in a comparable manner, the "system" has been characterized as unable to relate to them (Sanchez, 1974).

This inability to interrelate within the "system" is especially significant because meeting the needs of the elderly has, more and more, come to be seen as a responsibility of our "system" of government at Federal, State and local levels. Nationally enacted programs, operating with and through State and local agencies, are increasingly recognized as the primary means by which society can provide the assistance needed by its older citizens. If Hispanic or other minority elderly cannot relate to this structure or if the structure cannot relate to the needs of persons within such groups, little measurable progress in ameliorating adverse conditions can be expected.

In order to improve "system" responsiveness, and in recognition of the special circumstances of minority elderly, Congress has mandated that priority attention be given to meeting the needs of older persons in minority groups through programs operating under the Older Americans Act (OAA) and administered by the U.S. Administration on Aging (AoA) within the U.S. Department of Health, Education, and Welfare. In the absence of funds sufficient to guarantee program availability to all older persons, Congress has directed that the major service programs operating under this Act—Title III and Title VII programs—be designed to give priority attention to those elderly with the greatest economic and social need. For purposes of these programs, those in greatest need have been defined as minority and low-income individuals (low-income being defined as below the Bureau of the Census poverty threshold).

The OAA Title III program is designed to encourage and assist State and area agencies on aging to concentrate resources in order to develop greater capacity to foster the development of comprehensive and coordinated social service systems to serve older persons. Legislation authorizing the program was enacted in May 1973; rules and regulations governing its conduct were published in final form in October of that year. The OAA Title VII national nutrition program, the primary purpose of which is to provide older Americans with low-cost, nutritionally sound meals, was enacted into law in March 1972; final regulations were issued in August of that year.

This paper is devoted to an examination of the question of how we can begin to judge the extent to which these programs, after four to five years of operating experience, are achieving their expressed purpose of focusing priority attention on low-income and minority elderly. This paper also seeks to address specifically the degree to which minority elderly, especially Hispanic elderly, are realizing an equitable share of resources and are otherwise being granted priority consideration under Title III and Title VII programs.

What Constitutes Priority Attention?

In the absence of a commonly accepted definition of priority attention, it is fair to structure an assessment of the responsiveness of Title III and Title VII programs to Hispanic and other minority elderly in terms of the relevant objectives and guidelines set forth for these programs in the Federal regulations under which they operate. As such, assessing priority attention becomes operationally defined as assessing the extent to which the programs are operating in accord with their own rules and guidelines. Since Title III and Title VII regulations were issued after review and comment by interested individuals and organizations, it is assumed that there is common acceptance of the merits of their provisions, at least as minimal standards. These regulatory provisions for priority attention, as reported in the following sections, are drawn from published Federal regulations: namely, 45 CFR Part 903 and 45 CFR Part 909.

Provisions of Title III (45 CFR Part 903)

Title III grants for State and community programs on aging are distributed initially on a formula basis among the States according to each State's population aged 60 and over. The State agency designated by the Governor as the State agency on aging expends available funds in accord with its AoA-approved annual State plan. In turn, the State agency on aging makes funds available to State-designated area agencies on aging which represent and serve distinct planning and service areas. The latter may encompass a county, multi-county, metropolitan, or city area. Each area agency on aging expends its funds in accord with a State-approved annual area plan and is responsible for monitoring and assessing programs for which it makes funds available. The State agency may support activities and services in geographic areas not served by an area agency under an area plan.

Title III funds are made available primarily for use in planning (including data collection and analysis) and service coordination and as incentive funds designed to encourage and promote the availability and utilization of non-Title III financial resources in providing services to older persons. Direct Title III support for social services is available, although on a time-limited basis. Built into the program is the expectation that permanent funding will be found elsewhere for meritorious social service projects. In services funding, principal emphasis is placed on support for those social services, such as information and referral, outreach, and transportation, designed to aid older persons in gaining access to other types of supportive services and activities available in their communities. A wide range of other social services can be supported under Title III when it can be clearly shown that such services are needed, are not already available, and will not or cannot be provided by other public or private agencies. The Congressional mandate in the 1975 amendments to the Older Americans Act requires that these "gap-filling" services include some or all of a specific set of national priority services. These include transportation, home services (including homemaker-home health services), legal and other counseling services, and residential repair and renovation programs.

I. State Agency Requirements for Granting Priority Attention

In the conduct of the Title III program, beyond the objective of promoting the development of comprehensive, community-based service systems available and accessible to all older persons, provision is made to insure priority attention to minority elderly through the requirements placed on each State agency to:

- Identify the location, special needs, and living conditions of those older people in greatest need, with special attention to low-income and minority elderly.
- Analyze the needs and characteristics of such older persons and establish priority uses for available funds in accord with such analyses.
- Develop systems for the storage, retrieval, and analysis of the data collected and for dissemination of such data to public and private agencies as well as the public at large.
- Insure that an adequate number of qualified staff, including members of minority groups, are assigned full-time to assure effective conduct of State agency responsibilities.
- Develop and implement an affirmative action plan for equal employment opportunity, and make this plan available for public review upon request.
- Facilitate consumer participation in the development and implementation of the required annual State plan through:
  —periodic public hearings, with adequate public notice of intent to conduct such hearings.
  —establishment of a State committee to advise the Governor and the State agency, with one-half of the membership of this committee to be representative of older consumers, including

low-income older persons and minority elderly at least in proportion to the relative number of minority elderly in the State.

- Evaluate, on an ongoing basis, the extent to which existing public and private programs meet the needs of older persons, especially low-income and minority individuals; and, as part of this evaluation, annually update analyses of available services and resources.
- Assure that, in granting funds for activities and services in areas not under area plans on aging, approved proposals are designed to serve primarily low-income and minority elderly.
- Insure that all older persons have reasonably convenient access to information and referral services which include bilingual personnel and personnel capable of overcoming potential barriers in such cases where the service is directed to a population that presents special communications patterns, such as among Spanish-speaking elderly.

2. Area Agency Requirements for Granting Priority Attention

In the absence of funds sufficient to fund area agencies on aging in all planning and service areas, a State agency is required to give priority to support for those areas with concentrations or significant proportions of low-income and minority elderly. Once established, in order to focus priority attention on its resident minority and low-income elderly, an area agency is required to:

- Collect and disseminate information on the needs of the elderly in the planning and service area, with special attention to the needs of low-income and minority elderly. Available resources and services are to be inventoried and their effects evaluated.
- Grant priority support to those activities and services which will assist and benefit low-income and minority elderly and assure that, to the extent feasible and with respect to resources under the area plan, such elderly individuals will be served at least in proportion to their relative number in the planning and service area.
- Insure an adequate number of qualified staff, working full- or part-time, including members of minority groups.
- Facilitate consumer participation in the development and implementation of the annual area plan through:
  —periodic public hearings.
  —establishment of an advisory council, representative of program participants and the general public, and including low-income persons and minority group members at least in proportion to their number in the planning and service area (at least one-half of the membership of the council is to be representative of consumers).
- Provide that contracts or grants under the area plan will be operated by minority individuals, at least in proportion to their relative number in the planning and service area.
- Evaluate activities carried out pursuant to the area plan and elicit the views of older consumers in this evaluation.

Both State and area agencies are required to provide for continuous programs of public information specifically designed to assure that information about the programs and activities they carry out is effectively and appropriately promulgated throughout the State or area. Both State and area agencies must also be responsive to freedom of information provisions requiring that their respective annual plans, all required periodic reports on program activities, and all Federal and State policies relevant to program conduct, be made available for public review.

Provisions of Title VII (45 CFR Part 909)

Title VII is designed to provide older Americans with low-cost, nutritionally sound meals served in strategically located centers such as schools, churches, community centers, senior citizen centers, and other public or private facilities where they can obtain other social and rehabilitative services. The program is targeted on low-income persons who evidence certain psychological, physiological, and social conditions that make difficult the maintenance of proper nutritional health and social well-being. By definition, minority elderly are to be given special consideration in program activities.

Federal funds are distributed to States on a formula basis for this program, according to each State's population aged 60 and over. The State agency on aging makes project grant awards in accord with a Federally-approved annual State plan. Projects approved in accord with this plan must provide not only economical, nutritionally sound meals in convenient sites, but also must make provision for comprehensive and ongoing outreach activities from each meal site. Such outreach activities are to be designed to assure that the maximum number of hard-to-reach target group eligibles actually participate in the program. Projects must also provide ongoing public information activities designed specifically to inform target group eligibles of the services offered.

In addition, projects must provide for supportive social services to the extent that these services are needed and are not available or accessible to the individuals participating in the nutrition project. Up to 20 percent of a State's allotment can be used to support such services which include transportation and escort services, information and referral, health and welfare counseling, nutrition education, shopping assistance, and re-creation activities incidental to the project.

1. State Agency Requirements for Granting Priority Attention

Over and above the outreach and public information activities, Title VII regulations direct specific focus on granting priority attention to minority elderly through requirements that a State agency:

- Select areas for project awards in consideration of the number of minority group eligibles in such areas, in order to assure that of the total number of elderly served, minorities will be served at least in proportion to their number among the eligible individuals in the State.
- Make awards, to the extent feasible, to projects to be operated by minority individuals (or provide for subcontracts within awards) at least in proportion to their number among eligible individuals in the State.
- Develop and implement an affirmative action plan for equal em-

ployment opportunity and make such plan available for review upon request.
- Obtain advisory assistance (including review and advice on the State plan) from consumers of services, including representatives of minority groups.

2. Nutrition Project Requirements for Granting Priority Attention

Title VII projects are required to grant priority attention by insuring the presence of:

- Project staff who, to the extent feasible, are representative of the minority group individuals participating in the project.
- A project advisory council to advise on the delivery of nutrition services and to approve project policies related to such issues as the determination of menus to meet cultural and other dietary preferences of participants. More than one-half of the members of this council are to be consumers of services, representative of the meal sites involved in the project, and elected by site participants.
- Special menus, where feasible and appropriate, at each site to meet the particular dietary needs of participants arising from their health or religious requirements or their ethnic backgrounds.

Summary of Major Provisions for Priority Attention

To summarize the major provisions of the rather lengthy list of prescriptive rules and regulations, the granting of priority attention to minority elderly under the terms of Title III and Title VII programs requires that:

—State agencies on aging are to provide funding preference to project areas, nutrition sites, and planning and service areas with high concentrations or proportions of minority (and low-income) elderly.

—Minority elderly are to receive proportioned benefits. Under Title III area plans they are to be served at least in proportion to their relative number in the planning and service areas. Under Title VII the State agency is to assure that they are served at least in proportion to their number among eligible individuals in the State.

—Advisory assistance is to be secured from elderly consumers, including minority representatives. In program planning activities under Title III, minority elderly are to be represented on advisory committees to State and area agencies at least in proportion to their number in the State or planning and service area. Under Title VII, minority elderly are to advise the State agency and to serve on project advisory panels.

—State and area agency staff and nutrition project staff are to include minority representatives. Under Title VII, affirmative action plans for equal employment opportunity are specifically required in State agencies; nutrition project staff are expected to reflect the cultural makeup of project participants.

—Emphasis is to be placed on the provision of services—including outreach, information and referral, transportation and escort services—designed to assist needy older persons to gain access to and utilize existing programs and services. For information and referral services supported under Title III, bilingual staff are to be available to help persons take advantage of available benefits.

Has Priority Attention Been Granted?

Have Title III and Title VII programs achieved their expressed purpose of focusing priority attention on low-income and minority elderly? There seems to be no nationally applicable answer. On the one hand, the Administration on Aging (AoA), the Federal agency responsible for administration of Older Americans Act service programs, reports that State and area agencies and nutrition projects have made important strides forward in expanding the participation of low-income and minority elderly. On the other hand, State and area agencies, in a May 1976 study of their technical assistance needs, identify minority participation as a major area of program weakness (Administration on Aging, 1976).

Interestingly enough, the technical assistance needs report finds State and area agencies acknowledging that major barriers to effective provision of priority attention include:

—Inadequate information on the identity of minority and low-income elderly populations and their needs.
—Language barriers between staff and clients.
—Staff unfamiliarity with minority group cultures.
—Underrepresentation of minorities on program staff.
—Lack of culturally relevant services.
—Lack of appropriate outreach staff and media.
—Inadequate transportation for clients.
—Inappropriate site locations.
—Poor linkages between policy makers and program providers.
—Lack of enough minority subcontractors and training for them.
—Perceptions of minorities as lacking capabilities to develop acceptable funding applications and to operate programs.

Inasmuch as each of these identified barriers addresses an issue for which provision is made in formal program regulations, the conclusion to be drawn is that State and area agencies, in the aggregate, are experiencing limited success in meeting regulatory requirements to provide attention to minority elderly.

AoA reports that minority elderly receive services at least in proportion to their relative number in the older population. Minority elderly comprise approximately 10 percent of the older population; AoA reports that they constitute between 12 and 20 percent of the persons reported as participating in or benefiting from area agency activities under Title III. Under Title VII, approximately 22 percent of older people served in FY 1976 (that is, through March 30, 1976) were reported to be minority elderly. The adequacy of this numerical representation among program beneficiaries is circumspect, however, when it is considered that the poverty rate among minority elderly is twice that of the elderly white population and that other debilitating conditions associated with age are equally more prominent among minority elderly than among their white counterparts. Further doubt is raised as to the degree to which program activities reflect adequate efforts to grant priority attention.

Assessing the adequacy of priority attention efforts from another perspective, it is acknowledged that minority personnel among the staff of State and area agencies and nutrition projects exceed levels of representation proportional to their number in the population at large. In the aggregate, 17 percent of State agency professional staff are reported to be minority persons, as are 15 percent of area agency professional staff, and 30 percent of staff employed in nutrition projects. By their own reports, however, State and area agencies recognize that the presence of minority staff in such numbers has been insufficient to overcome barriers restricting minority group participation in their programs. As a result, one must ask if minority individuals have been hired in numbers sufficient to insure priority attention to the needs of minority elderly. One might also ask if the minority individuals employed to date have been placed in positions where they can effectively shape or influence improved program responsiveness to minority elderly or, as is suggested by the proportionately higher percentage of minority persons among nutrition project staff, are minority individuals more likely to be employed in service delivery roles as opposed to planning, resource utilization, evaluation, and policy making positions?

Are Hispanic Elderly Receiving Equitable Treatment?

From a national perspective, there appears to be no hard data available to evaluate the extent to which Hispanic elderly are receiving equitable treatment or priority attention under Titles III and VII. Statistical data on program participants and staff fail to distinguish among minority groups, but new program reporting procedures have been designed to overcome this deficiency. At the national level there are no data available to indicate the degree to which Hispanic consumers are represented on advisory and planning committees, the degree to which Hispanic individuals and organizations have benefited from minority contract and grant provisions, or the degree to which Title III and Title VII services, including "access" services, have focused on Hispanic elderly. The assumption is made, however, that the barriers, identified by State and area agency staff as limiting the participation of low-income and minority elderly in general, have specific application to Hispanic elderly.

Can More Be Done to Gain and Assess Priority Attention?

The Administration on Aging acknowledges that more can and should be done to insure that (1) special services are delivered to minority elderly, (2) minority individuals and organizations play a more active role in program planning, operation, and evaluation, and (3) a solid body of evaluative data is collected and maintained on the degree to which such objectives are being met. To this end, AoA has sought to institute a continuing program of technical assistance, consultation, data and information collection, and program assistance. During FY 1976, among other objectives, this program focused on providing policy direction and technical assistance ("how-to" methodologies) to State agencies, and through them to area agencies, in order to aid such agencies to increase (a) minority participation as beneficiaries of Titles III and VII, (b) affirmative action in equal employment opportunity, and (c) the provision of grants and contracts to minority organizations (Administration on Aging, 1975). As part of this strategy, AoA awarded a model project grant to the *Asociación Pro Personas Mayores* to enable that association to develop technical assistance tools and to provide consultation to State and area agencies on specific ways to improve programs and services on behalf of Hispanic elderly.

However, without de-emphasizing the importance of such efforts, three systematic conditions are recognized as limiting the pervasiveness of their effects. First, the minimal standards for priority attention were written into program provisions at the outset. If such standards have not been addressed in initial program planning and design efforts at the State and local level (and, in many cases, they obviously were not), then the conservative force imposed by established program operations must be overcome if such standards are to be met at this time. For example, initial project grants have been made, and projects are in operation. If such projects were not designed at the outset to focus priority attention on minority elderly, then special consideration must now be extended within the limits imposed by established program practices and operations.

Secondly, although time and efforts may reduce limitations introduced by existing operating modes, the additional barriers introduced by the limits of available resources are not so easily overcome. The fact is that as a matter of Federal policy we have not undertaken to guarantee the nationwide availability of the social and health-related services needed by the elderly or other dependent groups within the population (Beall, 1977). The level of funding available under both Titles III and VII is not sufficient to insure program availability even to those in greatest need. It has been estimated, for example, that to extend the benefits of the Title VII program alone to the estimated five million persons eligible for participation in it in 1973 would have cost $2 billion (Richardson, 1973). And, even with steadily rising appropriations, the FY 1977 appropriation for Title VII was only $203.5 million, thereby insuring that not all needs could be met. Because financial resources are so limited and a large number of competing demands are made for their use, there are no Federal guarantees of the availability of such resources in every community. Furthermore, the widespread dispersion of scarce program resources assures that, where funds are available, few projects will secure the level of funding necessary to develop and maintain comprehensive service programs. As a consequence, Titles III and VII should be seen as only a partial answer to meeting the needs of elderly persons and as an even less adequate single vehicle for responding to the debilitating effects of multiple jeopardy on the part of minority elderly.

The third systematic condition relates to the decentralized authority that exists under Title III and Title VII programs. State and area agencies, responding to State and local situations, operate under broad Federal guidelines in the conduct of programs. State and local responsiveness to minority interests will not result from Federal requirements alone, especially if these requirements are not strictly enforced. It might be expected, however, that State and area agencies, of necessity, would respond to the advocacy efforts of their respective constituencies. This supposition gives rise to the notion that well-organized advocacy efforts at State and local levels are needed in order to document the situation of minority elderly, identify means of meeting their needs, promote adoption of these means, and evaluate their adequacy. It might be expected that more equitable distribution of resources under Titles III and VII will occur when, together with strict enforcement of compliance with regulatory provisions for priority attention to minority elderly, minority elderly themselves and their representatives exert the influence necessary to alter the existing power structure and resource allocation patterns in their communities and States.

Postscript

Since this paper was completed, both Houses of the U.S. Congress, in proposed 1978 amendments to the Older Americans Act (H.R. 12255, House Report 95-1150; S. 2850, Senate Report 95-855), further address the issue of minority participation in Federally-assisted programs that affect older persons. The form in which this attention is given in amendments approved by both the House and Senate is a call for a study of racial and ethnic discrimination in these programs. The study, to be conducted by the U.S. Commission on Civil Rights, would give particular attention to identifying any Federal program in which evidence is found of persons being denied benefits or being excluded from participation on the basis of race or ethnicity.

This effort to "get at the facts" of racial and ethnic discrimination in programs for older Americans is commendable. But it is to be hoped that the proposed study takes a broad view of the question of what constitutes discrimination toward Hispanic and other racial/ethnic minority elderly. Judging the adequacy of program responsiveness to minority interests requires a consideration of issues broader than those presented by a study of the possible exclusion of one individual from a particular program or service. Should it not be judged discriminatory, for example, if a minority older person has few or no service programs in his or her neighborhood or community from which he or she could derive benefits? Or if services made available are not provided in a manner that not only respects, but also directly addresses his or her special cultural/linguistic needs and circumstances? Such a study should also consider questions related to the presence or absence among staff of persons with special sensitivities to older members of minority groups. The effects of poorly delivered services might be as adverse or as worse than having no access to services at all.

A further note of caution seems appropriate. A study of the type called for by the Congress allows attention to be focused on the problem of discrimination. Although welcome as a first step, it does not, in and of itself, insure the removal of discriminatory practices which are likely to be identified. This is especially true of such practices and barriers embedded in the present systems for planning and providing benefits and services. In short, the significance of the proposed study lies in the uses to which its findings are directed. Seeing to it that the findings are acted upon is the challenge that will confront those who represent and advocate for the interests of Hispanic and other racial/ethnic minority elderly.

REFERENCES

Beall, George Thomas. Financing the services: an assessment of the availability and application of Federal resources. *In* Wilma Donahue, Marie McGuire Thompson, and D.J. Curren (eds.), *Congregate Housing for Older People: An Urgent Need, A Growing Demand.* Washington, D.C.: Government Printing Office, 1977.

Brotman, Herman B. Every tenth American. *In* U.S. Senate, Special Committee on Aging, *Developments in Aging, 1974 and January-April 1975.* Washington, D.C.: Government Printing Office, 1975.

Richardson, Elliot R. The maze of social programs. *Washington Post,* Section C, 3, 21 January 1973.

Sanchez, Pablo. The Spanish-heritage elderly. *In* E. Percil Stanford (ed.), *Minority Aging: Proceedings of the Institute on Minority Aging.* San Diego, California: Center on Aging, School of Social Work, San Diego State University, January 1974.

U.S. Department of Health, Education, and Welfare, Administration on Aging. Operational planning system: fiscal year 1976, objective 1—building capacity of State (and Area) Agencies on Aging. Mimeographed memorandum, May 27, 1975.

_____ .*A Technical Assistance Guide for Directors and Personnel of Regional, State, and Area Agencies on Aging in the Implementation of Title III and Title VII Programs.* Prepared under contract by Health Facilities Resources, Inc., Washington, D.C., May 1976.